Ga g Rosebuds in Kerala

A Memoir About Storing Life's Special Moments

Peter Billingham

Randan Press

Randan Press

First edition independently published under the name - Randan Press 2022

Cover designed by Oliviaprodesign

ISBN – Hardback - 978-1-913911-23-2
ISBN – Paperback - 978-1-913911-22-5
ISBN - Large Print - 978-1-913911-24-9
ISBN - Dyslexia-Friendly Edition - 978-1-913911-29-4
ISBN – eBook - 978-1-913911-21-8

Typeset in - *EB Garamond* - Formatted on Atticus

This book is dedicated to
Paul Smith,
whose inspiration it was to write these stories,
and for being an inspiration.

Contents

To The Virgins, To Make Much Of Time

Gather ye Rose-buds while ye may,
Old Time is still a-flying:
And this same flower that smiles today,
Tomorrow will be dying.

The glorious Lamp of Heaven, the Sun,
The higher he's a-getting;
The sooner will his Race be run,
And nearer he's to Setting.

That Age is best, which is the first,
When Youth and Blood are warmer;
But being spent, the worse, and worst
Times, still succeed the former.

Then be not coy, but use your time;
And while ye may, go marry:
For having lost but once your prime,
You may forever tarry.

Robert Herrick, 1591-1674

Chapter 1

The Day It Began

I was 45 the day I became older than my dad.

That was the day it began. It was a day when the wings of reality smacked me hard in the face and woke me up to realising 'time is a-flying.' Not time in hours, days, and years, but in a life. My life. My unique, my one and only precious life.

From that day, possessions over experiences and occupations over relationships shifted. Looking back, that shift was in the smallest degree. But like two airplanes taking off from the same runway, each heading one degree apart in direction, with time, the separation between them widens until the distance between them is substantial. Worlds apart.

I feel a growing apprehension about getting older. The nearer the 'glorious Lamp' of my life has risen beyond the mornings of childhood and adolescence, beyond its zenith of middle age, and now in the afternoon of life, is closer to setting. Like it or not, today I will tick off another day – one less.

Everything around me is getting old. Atrophy. Even the word sounds uncomfortable to say. The unrelenting downward spiral. Inevitable endings. Everything that is alive is only heading in one direction. It's happening to those I love, my family, even my dog. To ignore it feels foolish. To fear it seems weak. But to embrace the passing days, is that even possible?

Is it possible to change my perspective on ageing?

If it was, it could help the surging growth of those around me who will be living well over 65. 'The Silver Tsunami' is surging towards the shores on the crest of an ageing population. Critics claim even using the term is ageist, but however you view it, the tidal 'Grey Wave' is coming in fast. By 2050, according to the United Nations, one in six people in the world will be over 65, while some 426 million will be over 80.

Many people try to find the elusive elixir of perpetual youth in a jar or under a knife. The goal it seems, is to not grow old, but remain looking young, as if there is no beauty in a face and body that has lived, and not just been alive. The marketing departments of cosmetic companies spend billions selling us that dream in pots of creams, or potions with serious-sounding names, but even the miracle cures yet undiscovered can't hold back ageing forever.

It's not like I'm trying to hold back the waves of time, Canute style. I'm not averse to the wrinkle lines on my face, the slight stoop in the walk, the silver hair – I'm happy to still have hair! But can I embrace it all? I am getting older each day, and nothing can stop that. Well, one thing can. The one thing that stops us getting older today is the one thing we don't want to face. The end of our days.

By occupation, I've had a unique insight into how many people's days end. More often than not, it is unexpected, and unprepared for. I've been writing about dead people in my role as a funeral celebrant and eulogy writer for over seven years. Through hundreds of conversations with people mourning the loss of a loved one, the stories, memories and thoughts they share with me come back time and time again to those special moments that mark their shared lives. Most often, it's not what you would imagine, and it's rarely the material rewards which are the pursuit of much of our lives.

When you have stood next to over 700 coffins telling the life story of the person inside, it makes you think about these things in deeper ways. Not just think but feel – emotional contagion is real. It can infect you with happiness and sadness just the same. The randomness and unexpectedness of death is disconcerting. Which makes life to me feel all the more treasured and precious. And limited.

So, over these last few years, preserving each day of my life has taken on a new meaning. Why? Because I've learned 'life' has this way of reminding us in those unknown, unexpected, and unprepared ways that our days do have a number. My remaining days are not known nor guaranteed, but they are numbered.

It leaves questions nagging in my mind: – how can I make the most of tomorrow, today, and the days that have passed? What if there was a perspective on life I could take that could make that relenting forward march of years feel different? How can I live in 'today' but find joy, happiness, and wisdom from 'yesterday?' How can my 'tomorrows' be filled with meaning and purpose? Is there any way to see my future is not contracting, but expanding? That I'm adding this today, and its unique memories and experiences, to a growing collection of other todays and not removing it from my supply of tomorrows?

Adrian Mole was 13 and 3/4 when he wrote his secret diary. I am fifty-nine and heading well towards sixty. This is not a diary, and my age is not a secret. Sixty sounds so much older than fifty-nine. I'm close to hitting 'three score years,' and wondering what the 'then' and beyond (optimistically) might look like.

I will never be young again. My back and legs, in a whisper that is growing louder, remind me of that unwelcome news each morning putting on a pair of socks. Young, you get a painful twinge in your knee, or ache in your back. Too much gardening or lifting, perhaps. After a few days, it disappears like the Spring morning mist burnt off by the sun. Now, those same aches and pains stay all day.

The standard image they present in media and culture is growing old gracefully (or disgracefully) is not something to anticipate with relish. Any good looks you once noticed in the mirror each morning have long gone. There are more mechanical devices you put on your body for the bits that don't work so well anymore. I take longer to remove these than my clothes these days when it is time to get into bed.

Something within me is fighting against that. There is a youthful voice of resistance crying deep within that never seems to grow old, no matter how long I live. There is still an unquenchable fire of desire to discover, learn, and explore burning within. What is this force keeping the spirit of life flaming bright within? Whatever it is, it is the one thing I want and hope will be the last thing to go.

I don't want it to sound that I'm getting maudlin. I'm not. I realise that there are more days behind than ahead for me. I understand that. But I am planning for many more years ahead. My mum has thirty more years on me. I'm not older than my mum yet.

There is no bargain you can make with life on its length. It's not like a guaranteed contract – even 'three score years and ten' are not a guarantee. I'm grateful for this day, but do deeply understand it is one less for me.

I think it wise to face mortality straight in the eye and say ... well, there are a few things I'd say to Father Time or The Grim Reaper. But let me declare fading away gracefully and giving up on adventures is not my style or choice. Why, when potentially there are so many more adventures ahead? Why not stoke that fire burning within?

I am fifty-nine and three quarters. I'm going to celebrate the impending arrival of sixty in advance by traveling to India with my wife, Noreen. It has been a dream to visit India, and it's about to happen. I want to fully embrace everything I find there – the culture, the people, the food and anticipate along the journey, I'll gather a few more special memories – what I think the poet Robert Herrick called 'Rose-buds,' I shall call rosebuds, to store away for my future. But I'm getting ahead of my story.

I'm also doing it for another reason. As we age, we remember those things we choose to pay attention to. I want intentionally to remember the adventures of my life. So, I'm embarking on an Indian adventure.

Chapter 2

Do Not Pass Go

Time stands still in an airport. Whatever time of day it is, it's always OK to have a pint of John Smith's at Wetherspoons. Then they call your flight, and it's the mad rush to drink up and get to the gate. Bit like old age. You think you've got all the time in the world to drink your beer, then suddenly you feel the need to hurry as the bar of life is closing and an angelic voice is calling time.

Getting from home to Kerala, India, was a simple hop on two Emirates flights, Birmingham to Dubai (impressive airport) and then Dubai to Cochin International. Airports never lose their fascination and excitement. I worked in Kiev, Ukraine for an International Charity, commuting there every other week from the UK. You'd think after flying 8-10 times a month for seven years, airports would lose the appeal. Not for me. It signals the beginning of an adventure.

Disconcerting is the number of people around us travelling with face masks. Signs on walls and doors were asking if we were returning from China or Italy. We were not, so we were unconcerned – then.

There is a sick feeling as the plane starts its descent. It's not because I can see the view the pilot sees on the in-flight entertainment system, it's a fearful nagging question in my guts. All the planning, research, emails, and calls in advance, was it enough? The nauseating sensation in the pit of my stomach is more wondering if 'Pete's DIY Tours' can bring it all together as planned. With my pockets full of the little bottles of 'Dutch courage' I'd helped myself to off the drinks trolley as it went past, I felt like shouting at the top of my voice – 'Bring on the rabid dogs, I've had my injections. I've got enough Imodium for a packet a day. Let the birthday adventure begin!'

The world is small. I'm fifteen hours from home and here in India. Six degrees of separation, they say. We are not that distanced from the beauty or uprising, majesty or turmoil of another human being. 'Over there' is really close. The troubles of the world are troubles for us all.

It's funny the way time differences play havoc with your body. My legs think it is 2:00 am, but my head is struggling to grasp local time is 7:30 am. We need to move. We need to get cash. Currency restrictions prevent taking rupees into India. No problem. According to 'The Plan' there are ATMs in the arrival hall. There were – a singular. Only one.

A queue of other bleary-eyed travellers ahead is discovering what I would soon know – it is not working. A row of 'currency exchange' booths is the only option. Like fresh meat on the Serengeti, the pack dive in.

Tip one: should you ever be in Cochin International Airport, the ATM not working (perhaps it never does) and forced to use a currency exchange booth, have cash, preferably dollars. I didn't. The conversion rate for currency exchange using a foreign currency bank card that should have gone in the ATM was about as advantageous as letting hedgehogs play in a bouncy castle.

I withdraw enough money using their currency exchange card machine for a couple of days. 'The Plan' says there are ATMs everywhere in India, so I'm not too worried. In return, there is a thick bunch of notes being pushed across the counter towards me. Foreign currency always reminds me of Monopoly money when you first see it. I stash the wads of cash safely away.

Behind me stands a most distinguished looking 'gent' wearing a cream linen jacket, striped shirt, red chinos, and deck shoes. He looks like he could be in a photoshoot for Country Life – The Cotswolds edition. He points to the large denomination notes the cashier is trying to give him with his Panama hat, the same notes the cashier had put in my hand, now in my back pocket. 'Don't give me those things,' he said. He knows something I don't. The cashier reluctantly swaps them for what looks like the winnings from 'Passing Go' and the rent on Mayfair and Park Lane with a hotel combined. He puts them into his wallet. I see the name of an upmarket travel company on his cases. I'm still wondering what the problem was with the notes I have as we head for the exit doors past more bleary-eyed tourists queuing up at the broken ATM.

Then the early morning heat hits us.

I've run many arrival hall gauntlets, crowds touting and eyeing you up as 'fresh fodder' for taxi drivers, tour guides, and scam artists of all kinds. Every airport seems to have those awaiting rich pickings from the new tourists arriving.

Exiting the airport terminal doors was not the manic experience I was expecting. It was almost disappointing. Instead, a sea of white-shirted smiling faces were looking expectantly towards the new arrivals. I see a sign saying, 'Mr Peter and Mrs Noreen.' I think that must be us. On 'The Plan,' I had booked an airport arrival taxi from our first hotel. Following the white shirt and the smile, and getting giddy from watching the waggling head going side to side, we climb into a clean, white Suzuki taxi. So far so good. Let's hope he takes us to the correct hotel.

From the depths of freezing Siberia in Russia to a busy international metropolis, and on to short 'hop and flop' holiday resorts in Europe, most roads as you leave airports are the same the world over. Billboards, rent a car garages, and random office blocks line wide tarmac roads heading away from the airport terminal. I always have a feeling of optimism as I pass by, heading on to awaiting adventures. However, with one unique difference – surrounding here are fields and fields of solar panels. Cochin International Airport is the only airport in the world that runs entirely on solar power.

Leaving the airport behind on wide modern dual carriageways, the roads begin to narrow and the traffic increases. Urban gives way to countryside. Staring out into the chaotic busyness of rural life, my mind crackles with excitement and anticipation.

I'm here. I'm in India!

Chapter 3

Why India?

When people think of India, it is with chaotic streets scenes, blaring horns, crowded banks of fast-flowing holy rivers the colour of liquid mud teeming with devotees fighting to get to the water's edge to appease one deity among the millions of gods they serve. India is mysterious temples, the curling smoke of incense rising upwards, like an invisible hand writing mysterious words in midair with unseeing fingers. Spicy food, but not suffering 'Delhi belly' (a global travel ailment whose name I would imagine is an affront to anyone who comes from Delhi) but packing copious packets of Imodium to offset it just in case.

Is that the real India? My India feels deeper, richer, and personal, like a friend I have yet to meet. Its image has grown in me over the years, layer upon layer, by experiences and observations, but much more by the people I have met. That's why it feels so personal, and human; those relationships painted a masterpiece in my mind imagining what I will find there.

My India is the India of attending history lectures at Birmingham University.

Aged 34, with the rest of the class about 18, my shiny new students' union card proclaimed me to be a full-time 'mature student' (I've never liked that term). I'd become disillusioned and exhausted by long stressful days. Curiosity led me on a quest to discover if someone who left school with few qualifications (read none) could succeed in academia. Recently resigned from a position of perceived authority and prestige, the crisp white business card with yellow and black embossed script that once lined my pocket defined me as the Senior Branch Manager for a major insurance company sales force. Now I'm about to start a three-year degree at Birmingham University to study Humanities, specifically theology, history, and English Literature. It was a shock to my ego. The old job was no position of any status at all as far as anyone there was concerned. That is why I'm sitting alone in the front row of the history lecture, enraptured. For some reason, everyone else sat at the back. It soon appeared that other students were not quite so eager as me to discover answers.

I was observed with suspicion and not some derision by the rest of the students, most who were not far off half my age. We would have group exercises. I was back again at school when they picked kids to play in sports teams. I was always the last one picked – 'OK, you can have Billingham.' That low and discarded position changed forever one day when we had to give a presentation in front of fellow students and lecturers.

Like that famous newspaper advert declared – 'They Laughed When I Sat Down At The Piano – But When I Started to Play!' I got up and delivered a powerful presentation on the Human Genome Project. Almost bringing them to tears, the soundtrack to Jurassic Park humming in the background in time with the PowerPoint slides, I don't think they had ever seen anything like it before. From then on, everyone wanted me in their discussion groups when it needed a presentation. Most of them were fearful of public speaking themselves, happy to pass the task on to me.

My fellow learners ganged up on me at the end of a lecture one day early on. They said, 'Stop asking questions at the end of lectures.' I said, 'Why?' 'You are keeping everyone else from heading to students' union bar.' Enough said. They never stopped me asking questions. Adoring three years of studying, and graduating with a First-Class Honours Degree, forever answered my quest and curiosity.

It was in history lectures I learned of the rise and ruin of the East India Company. How when East India Company officials and employees returned with tales of this mysterious land and its exotic peoples it increased the development of racism and white supremacist beliefs in Europe. Dissolved by an act of Parliament in 1873, the layers of bureaucracy and trade systems established by the East India Company remained in place through the years of the British Raj. The Indian Civil Service would build administration systems deep into the culture of the nation, along with the railways and a legal system that took minor consideration of the multifaith population. British rule would end with the partition of India.

It was through the passionate teaching of one young professor at Birmingham University, who brought to life the intricacies and scheming of politicians of the partition of India. No dusty history for her, The Radcliffe Line separated her family, splitting the generations apart like an earthquake creates fissures in land. A line dividing a nation separating faiths, a line drawn on a map that left a million people dead. This era of Indian history consumed my studies for a year. It left me with an appreciation and wonder of the people of India. A wonder seeding a dream that one day I want to see some of this mysterious and magnificent nation for myself.

My India is the many people I've met and worked with over the years whose heritage is Indian.

The stories they told of village life before coming to England, and of grandparents still there, captivated me. Working alongside sales associates and sales managers with Asian roots deep in India and Pakistan taught me about their faiths, customs, and values. I was a diligent student, curious about arranged marriages, regular temple visits, the festivals they enjoyed, and the expansive and expensive weddings saved for since the day their daughters were born.

They introduced me to the food – spicy curries from Madras and baltis from Kashmir. It planted seeds – and gave me indigestion! There were many invitations to travel to their home villages, meet their families, and soak up the culture. That was then, and my answer was no. The time not right, the family too young. Or was it?

That's the other reality you think about at fifty-nine and three quarters – missed opportunities. The choice you could have taken to experience adventures in life, but somehow 'life' and 'busyness' got in the way. You can't do anything about yesterday. But this is now, this is today. Sixty is approaching at warp speed.

My India is the India of TV travel programmes.

Regal Joanna Lumley, a prerequisite silk scarf tied perfectly at her neck, being swooned over by the remnants of stately maharajas in pink palaces on luxury jaunts to Jaipur. The India of Rick Stein and The Hairy Bikers cooking curry by the roadside as gaggles of smiling children look on, their parents' waggling heads vying for a better position in the background. My India is the India of films, the epic Gandhi, or the delightful The Best Exotic Marigold Hotel awakening and nurturing the delights that India could offer an 'oldie' like me.

So that's it. I'm off to see if my India is the real India. With the big birthday approaching, and the decision now made, the next question was, where in India do we go?

There are a lot of places to choose from in India! The classic tourist route – The Golden Triangle – would take us to Jaipur, Delhi, and Agra. That was appealing for the history, iconic views, and the India many tourists see. 'Pete's DIY Tours' spent a considerable time researching that option. Organising an Indian tour on that route was possible, but something was nagging at me about being independent tourists in India on our own, so to speak.

Was independent travel to India a step too far, even for 'Pete's DIY Tours'? Did I now need to find a travel agent that could help me? The magnitude of the cities, and fearing the teeming reality of visiting places, and palaces overrunning with tourists fighting to get the Princess Diana Taj Mahal photo moment could shatter my dream of India.

There was of course the destination of the hippy trail in the 1960s – Goa on the West coast. Laid-back culture, cheap food, and inexpensive accommodation sounded appealing. But reading about some of the experiences I could find there, perhaps if it was my thirtieth birthday, and I enjoyed a good full moon beach party, it would have been ideal. Maybe not Goa then.

Instead, my eyes were drawn further South down the map of India. Describing the area as a peaceful visual treat for the eyes, its long empty sandy beaches, lazy backwaters and natural beauty devoid of crowds on well-worn tourist routes, made it sound perfect.

Decision made then – we're off to Kerala!

Chapter 4

God's Own Country

Kerala sits between the pristine turquoise waters of the Arabian Sea on the West and tiered tea plantations nestling along the Western Ghat Mountains to the East. The Kerala landscape is fast-flowing rivers and lazy backwaters where reed houseboats saunter along narrow canals overgrown with water hyacinths. The canals feeding the rice fields either side make everywhere verdant, vibrant, and lush. Kerala is mountainside tea plantations, thick forests, and shorelines of empty white sandy beaches. Kerala is laid-back, relaxed, less frantic and crowded. The more I learned about the area the less the hesitation of organising an independent tour grew, though it didn't disappear completely. It made this part of India captivating and inviting.

In 1989 Walter Mendez was Corporate Creative Director at the national Indian advertising agency Mudra Communications. Given the task by the Kerala Tourism Department to promote and develop tourism in the region, he wrote the tagline – 'God's Own Country' – Kerala. It stuck. It's worked wonders for developing a constant flow of tourists from then on to wonder in awe and majesty at the beauty and diversity within the landscape, religion, and people. I'm not sure which or whose God 'owns' Kerala, as Hindus, Muslims, and Christians live together without conflict and in religious tolerance of each's faiths. For the last 30 years tourism increased, but the region still remained the welcoming hospitality location Europeans found 500 years before.

In the 3rd century BCE, an explorer found ancient rock inscriptions recording the name Ketalaputo, which became modern-day Kerala. The region's heritage in Indian history is one of royalty – the Chera dynasty. They were once one of the greatest of the four kingdoms in India. Rich in spices more valuable than gold, Kerala began international trading with Europe, the Red Sea region, and the Far East.

In 1498, Vasco da Gama established a sea route to Kerala, and the Portuguese arrived, along with the Dutch, French, and British in the guise of the East India Company, all signposting the beginning of the colonial era for Kerala. As these foreigners arrived, they brought with them their religions and cultures, shaping Indian society on the caste system. The British Raj expanded the discriminative caste order further. I can understand why. This unjust practice, when it arrived, transformed into a religious and cultural institution. The princely rulers of the kingdom and the enthusiastic arriving missionaries set up schools and promoted education, leaving a legacy making Kerala have the highest literacy levels in India today.

The ancient port city of Muziris became the gateway to India for foreigners arriving in previous centuries. So it seemed a perfect location for our first stop as well. Jews, Greeks, and Romans, followed by Portuguese, Dutch, and British, arrived by long and dangerous sea routes in search of trading spices and, finding them, became rich. Now two other Brits who arrived by Emirates Airlines and are bumbling along in small white Suzuki taxi in search of adventure. I wonder if they will find those riches there just as much?

Chapter 5

Thump-thump

OUR FIRST STOP IS a small hotel situated in a historic mansion. The location and setting are beautiful. Inviting rope hammocks swing between tall coconut palms that curve gently up and out over the Periyar River, which flows smoothly past us and out to the sea. Everyone here never stops smiling. Smiles seem to come easily, though perhaps life is not so easy for many – I see two gardeners are picking up leaves by hand. We follow our bags to the room upstairs. A wraparound balcony looks out over simple gardens bordering the river. The pair of swans shaped out of two towels, tiny rose petals for eyes, swim off the bed with a swift kick as we finally collapse into sleep.

It's early afternoon but feels like the morning after. Thump-thump my head throbs in time with the burr of the air conditioning – not from the bottles of 'Dutch courage,' but the pulling of jet lag.

We meander along the lane leading away from the old mansion house, past dilapidated buildings interspersed by rather grand homes. Shacks and mansions are side by side. Building materials of all shapes and quantities stack high in front gardens, hanging around like layabouts on street corners, not wanting to move or use their time well.

A group of road workers are thumping pickaxes into concrete. It is past midday, and the sun burns hot on our hatless heads. They stop swinging. Rather than it being my curiosity for the first encounter we have in India, it is us that becomes the curio. The stares from bright white eyes set back in black skin smile but leave me with the distinct feeling that few people venture out of those high protective gates – and not on their first afternoon, and not just for a stroll. Motioning to one man how hot he must be, he smiles back. He doesn't have a clue what I am trying to communicate. He nods and waggles his head and smiles again. The pickaxes remain silent as we saunter further along the lane – we feel white eyes following us.

We pass a large school with a Hindu temple in the playground. Ganesh, the remover of obstacles, is watching guard over the children. Around the shrine are offerings: new and old, clean and rotten.

We soon realise tourists don't venture this way. It's the back roads of a small rural community. We remain articles of curiosity to everyone that passes us, many perched on powerful motorbikes. Already I recognise the gentle heartbeat thump-thump of a Royal Enfield Bullet. Once the pride of Redditch not too far from where I live, they seem very popular here. Three-wheel tuk-tuks and mopeds speed past, driving on their horns nonstop. Through the palm trees on either side of the road, we see the odd backwater canal. Tied to the trunks are ancient wooden canoes, and a few thin cows secured much like the canoes so they won't wander far.

Arriving back at the hotel, a Mancunian accent with a beaming smile greets me. 'Have you sent your order out for beer?' he says. He could have been offering me the six numbers for Saturday night. 'How do we do that?' I say. Most hotels and homestays are dry. Licensing laws and religious observance restrict selling alcohol in Kerala. You can only buy alcohol from government-approved shops. Although I had been looking, I hadn't seen one yet. He had the keys to the kingdom, and he was offering to share them with me. Pointing to one of the staff, he says, 'Ask him, he hops into his car and heads to a local bar and comes back with an ice-cold Kingfisher beer,' he says. The young man, not speaking a word of English, but fluent in the universal sign language of drinking a beer, nods and waggles his head. I hand him enough money to buy me two hotels on The Angel Islington, and possibly enough for Fenchurch Street Station as a backup. Returning with our supplies shortly later, I give him the extra rupees change for his trouble, realising later it was probably a day's pay. No wonder he looked happy with his tip! Now I understand Cotswolds Man – small denomination notes are very handy.

The first evening meal was a feast! We ordered one each and as soon as they arrived we realised it was a mistake. Fortunately, we could wash them down with cold Kingfisher beers.

Our tired legs gently thump upwards on the stairs to our room. We take a moment together on the balcony, pinching ourselves, grateful and unbelieving we are here in India.

Before sleep finally overcomes me, pulling out my notebook and pencil and writing at the top of the page 'Day One', I begin gathering rosebuds.

Chapter 6

A Rosebud By Any Other Name

What are the 'Rose-buds' Herrick the poet so implores us to gather while we may?

Rosebuds are experiences that stop you in your tracks. Those singular and recurring times in life that make you catch your breath. Those moments you want to freeze frame forever. You can find them at first kisses and wedding altars. It is not uncommon to find rosebuds in maternity wards – I found two there. Often they appear in unexpected places, striking you with awe, like how an unforeseen vista breaking open before you blindsides you with its majesty. Or when perhaps you have seen the same scene hundreds of times before, but all of a sudden, in this moment, you see it as if for the first time. A moment of wonder available to be gathered and stored away. It's a feeling like an enfolding hug draping around your shoulders when you are least expecting it. That's a rosebud moment.

For me, rosebuds can be catching sight of a dawn breaking. The way morning mist hangs like horizontal curtains a few feet above the ground. Walking through the gossamer shimmer as it disappears around me without trace. Those mornings when breath streams from your mouth like the chimney on a steam train. Cloudless blue skies, the crunch underfoot of grass hardened by brilliant white frost sounding like the snap of a biscuit or the crunch of an apple. Or at the other end of a day, the sun setting, blood-red, soaking from the evening sky into the sea and bleeding its majesty across the waves; the horizon sucking the life from my day and giving it to others who live in lands to the East.

Rosebud moments filter past all the rubbish of the day, the worries that, on later reflection, never mattered anyway. Intentionally gathering them reminds me the world is more significant than the space occupied with my physical presence. It's greater than the years and days of my life. Getting older, and gathering these moments, slows down the speed it seems life is passing by. They remind me of days gone past, they bring joy in this day, and they will sustain my tomorrows. Rosebuds are a moment of transcendence. They are pieces of a jigsaw. Separate, they are only a glimpse of a whole. But if I could look at the completed picture, do they become my life? To this point, am I my collection of gathered rosebuds?

The experiences of my life make me me. Who I am and who I think I am today is the culmination of the experiences of my life. It is the story of me. Yes, there are a collection of genes inherited, opportunities missed and taken, mistakes made, successes celebrated, and the culture I was fortunate to be born into. But as I try to navigate the waters of change looking for the route to positive ageing, I'm finding I'm spending an increasing amount of time reflecting on these 'moments', the rosebuds of my life. That's what happens as you age; you spend increasing amounts of time remembering.

Rosebuds are found in our episodic memories. That part of our incredible storage system in our brain that recalls specific events, situations, and experiences. The beauty of them is that they are unique to us as we remember the 'me' in them. It may have been a normal event for someone else, but because it happened to me, and it's layered with emotion, it takes on significant meaning for me. The sunset I watched sink into the sea hand-in-hand was the same sunset for many, but not for us – it was a unique moment, a 'rosebud' moment. It's not just another sunset. It becomes the essence of the story of my life. And the more experiences, and the more I gather those into my episodic memory, the more I will have to sustain my life in the future.

Br. David Steindal-Rast is an American Catholic Benedictine monk, well known for his inspiring TED talk on living with gratitude and the benefits it brings into our life. He provided the narration to a video by Louie Schwartzberg called, 'A Good Day.' From the first time I watched this on YouTube and heard his gentle voice imploring me to open my eyes and see the uniqueness of the sky at this moment, it stirred something soul-deep within me. We can take for granted the beauty around us without realising that the sky we gaze up into will never look precisely this way again. It is a moment universally for everyone, but for me individually. The art of gathering rosebuds is spotting these exceptional moments in an ordinary day, what we might call an ordinary life. But is there ever such a thing as an ordinary life? I don't think so. Each life is extraordinary. Each life is unique and precious.

Rosebuds are intensely personal and yet common to all, both individual and universal. The first kiss is my first kiss. How I experience the same event that millions have experienced before is unique to me. They are me, my story, my life.

Rosebuds can not only be found in places; they dwell as much in people.

People the world over are the same. Everyone needs love, everyone needs the acceptance of being noticed and made to feel they make a difference somehow, to someone. To experience emotional connection with someone, even a stranger from another culture or continent, someone who can't utter the same spoken language as you, and recognising they have the same humanity within them, and you find some way to connect across the barriers of language – that's a rosebud for me as well. Most people in the world are kind and would help someone in trouble. Most humans want and enjoy sharing the days of their lives with others. Of course, that isn't always the case. I don't wander through life with 'rosebud' coloured spectacles. But I try to look for the good in people around me. And more often than not, I'm rewarded by finding it.

The benefit of writing over 700 eulogies is the lifetimes of stories I get to hear. Rosebuds come to me in the form of writing stories of triumph, and of love. They form the redemptive arc of a humble beginning turned into a glorious end. It might not be rags to riches in possessions, but the priceless wealth of building a family among the tragic relentless march of suffering that for many life endures. Overcoming, resilience, and the sheer guts to carry on. Those are wonderful and rewarding stories to write. Finding other stories in an extraordinary life sometimes don't appear so easy.

Each funeral is sad. The saddest are families who understand pieces are missing from the jigsaw of their family life. One of the saddest sentences I hear is, 'I wish I'd asked my mum and grandma about their lives when I had the chance.' Our family history and lives make up the picture on the jigsaw box with stories short and sweet, epic and mystifying. When you become aware events, experiences, and personalities are missing, it's like looking at an unfinished puzzle, knowing you will never be able to find the missing pieces. At that point in our conversation, I sense a profound regret from families being unable to answer the questions I ask.

As Hemingway famously said, most people don't listen. We can hear, but not listen. Often conversations are only opportunities waiting to get our story across, and not asking those open-ended questions that give space for another's rosebuds to be heard. If we only listened more to others and the stories of their lives, we'd realise rosebuds can be shared. If I hold space for another person to be heard, I water their garden of rosebuds. While their experience can't be mine, I get to walk among the garden of their days. But only if I'm willing to give them the unselfish gift of listening to them.

Rosebuds can sometimes be found in possessions. These gems are rarely in what we buy, more in what we have been given, passed on to us often by someone we loved, even maybe removed from us by a generation or so. Watch an episode of The Repair Shop on BBC to see how much the connection with a rosebud can be bound up in the worn-out fur of an old teddy bear, the ripped and fraying leather purse, or a broken toy. I have a couple of rosebuds like that in my collection - a letter opener brought in Switzerland, when money was in short supply, but dreams and the future held hope and promise. Along with a silver topped cane, discovered among the ruins of a deserted attic when a childhood home was being demolished.

Rosebuds are laughter and tears, happiness and sadness, those moments when you feel life is worth living. We can be blind to the rosebuds surrounding us and filling our days. Rosebuds are everywhere. We should look hard for them mixed in with ordinary and extraordinary days of our lives. It is not a passive activity but a proactive necessity. While we have the time to stop and take the trouble to notice them, rosebuds are there for the gathering. But that's the thing – we can miss them, overlook them, forget them and, when we get older, feel regret not gathering rosebuds when we had the opportunity. I think we can be blinded to seeing them in our younger years when it may seem other priorities consume our hours. I started to notice them more when I became older than my dad.

There are many times when I didn't intentionally gather the rosebuds that were around me. I think I was blinded by busyness. It was self-imposed busyness crowding my view of the wealth of those moments while I was ticking items off a to-do list. Far too many occasions present physically but absent mentally. Looking at a view but thinking about the next insurance sale, wondering how to cram one more activity into an already overworked schedule for the following day. Looking in on sleeping children, whispering goodnight, meetings taking priority over people again and again. I regret that so much. Yet, there among those once missed opportunities, are many moments I remember, and writing those memories today breathes life into yesterday. I am finding redemptive rosebuds can be there for gathering just as much.

That's the thing about rosebuds; you can suddenly wake up and realise you're missing out on gathering them. The doctor asks you to come back for more tests. You start attending funerals of close friends and people you know the same age as you. A near-miss in an accident, a close call in a hospital bed. I've seen life turn to a frantic harvest for some and for others they never started planting. Fallow fields lie empty of rosebuds.

I think it's true people never say on their death bed, 'I wish I had spent more time in the office.' Or, 'I wish that I had spent more time on Facebook reading about other people's rosebuds.' Actually, that's not true – most people who are 'intentional gatherers' don't post them on Facebook, they are too busy filling their limited days with memorable experiences, conversations, and reflections. Those saddest conversations I have writing eulogies seem to be for those lives who never intentionally gathered rosebuds.

Places, people, and possessions – who can judge what is one person's rosebud and another's thorn?

Rosebuds can be selective, and they can be an imperfect recollection of a moment, but that doesn't matter. We do edit our memories. I'm not sure I agree with author William Maxwell, who betrays this editing as falsehoods – 'talking about the past we lie with every breath we draw,' he writes. Yet, we can forget the thorns and remember the petals. Each time we retrieve a memory it can, however, grow, expanding the joy of the moment.

I've reached fifty-nine and three quarters, and I understand now more than ever I need to gather rosebuds in my todays. To notice them when I find them. To be mindful of this moment, the way the sky looks right now, the way the sun reflects off the water in a million diamond glints. Because I know I will need them and be thankful for them one day in the future.

I now intentionally choose to create experiences over owning possessions to give rise to the opportunity for gathering rosebuds. That's why, to celebrate my coming sixtieth birthday, I'm here in Kerala, India.

Chapter 7

Small but Beautiful

There is a sepia quality to the early morning light over the Periyar River. My first cup of coffee each morning tastes good anywhere. Yet looking over the water, watching the mist rise and a new day arriving, is a blessing I'm incredibly grateful to experience with this cup of coffee today. A rosebud for the gathering.

Smiling faces around me greet the day as they pick up every leaf blown off the trees last night by hand. They sweep the sand paths smooth. The same they do every day. Wages here for these staff are around £4 a day. I'm grateful for these people, but know I'm here in an oasis of calm amid lives of uncertainty and limited opportunities – a worrying dichotomy. It is not lost on me the fine balance between the benefits that tourism brings and how it affects local people who call this land home. Some experiences here will make me face that challenge head-on.

The waiter brings scrambled eggs for me and 'masala' omelette for Noreen. 'Not too much spice!' Breakfast consumed with more excellent coffee when we are told that our driver and guide have arrived to take us on our tour by tuk-tuk.

Outside the reception doors are two casual but smartly dressed men. They greet us with welcoming smiles and squeeze us into the back of a white tuk-tuk to explore the lost ports of the Muziris. It is a modern tuk-tuk. I'm disappointed, to tell the truth. Snow white – I imagined daffodil yellow. Four wheels – I'd dreamed three.

It's funny how sometimes you build a dream in your mind. Then it's not quite like what you thought it would be? Can reality steal rosebuds?

Shirley Valentine is one of my favourite plays (and films) by Willy Russell. Sitting alone in the moonlight by the edge of the sea, the dream she has held so close for so long wasn't a bit like the reality. No feeling serene or lovely, only regretting a 'little life' that would be over pretty soon. All those feelings given by God lost in an 'unused life.'

I don't hold the thought for long, but I had imagined yellow and three wheels. I quickly catch the thought and say to myself, 'Don't let one wheel rob the rosebuds from your hands, Pete.' I wonder, how many rosebuds have fell to the ground over my life, 'little or large,' being too blind to see the reality was different, but often better than the dream?

Our guide is slight of build, and gentle, his warm voice as soft as silk. He tells me his name; it has numerous syllables. It sounds like water rippling over pebbles when he repeats it to me for the third or fourth time. Seeing I don't understand him, he says, 'Most people call me Simon.' Simon speaks excellent English. I ask him where he learned to speak such colloquial English. 'It is self-taught with the aid of books and listening to English radio programmes,' he says. Simon comes from a small village 30 km away and has been a tour guide for the last twenty years. Before then, he was a news journalist, a fascinating story he tells me later.

As we set off, I lean forward and say, 'Please take us places where you rarely take tourists.' A conversation ensues between driver and guide in fast-paced Malayalam. This sounds more like whitewater rapids on the Zambezi. Lurching forwards, we head down twisting and turning narrow lanes parallel to the river, the horn never stopping.

The smooth pavementless tarmac is wide enough for one vehicle (four or three wheels) and, at a push, one motorcycle. At times, a miracle takes place. An approaching car, three mopeds carrying a total of ten passengers. and us pass side by side as coconut palms breath in letting the hoard pass physically unscathed but mentally traumatised. Well, at least the two passengers in the back of the modern white tuk-tuk.

Hidden under and between those coconut palms are self-build houses. Some are grand mansions, wide verandas and tiled entrances; others are concrete shacks. We see the odd cow tied up here and there. Different to other parts of India, they eat them in Kerala. Simon is looking out at the houses and says more than a few times, 'And observe, small but beautiful houses.'

Turning a sharp right-hand bend a few feet from the edge of the river, now glad we have four and not three wheels on the tuk-tuk, Simon asks the driver to stop and we get out. He points out particular spice and fruit trees. As the journey progresses, this happens so many times that I can't remember them all. But among the trees were cardamom, mangos, nutmeg, cinnamon, pepper, and 'triffids'; I do not know what he called them even after he told me three of four times.

Across the road from one stop, a grandfather and a grandson are fishing. They are sitting on a palm trunk sweeping out, their feet a few inches above the water. We smile and say, 'Hi,' and they greet us with smiles bright and welcoming in return. No fish yet, but hopefully, translates Simon from my questions. We are slowly walking back up the road towards the driver and tuk-tuk when suddenly the young boy comes racing after us, proud of his lunch now hanging from the simple rod in his hand.

We twist and turn around narrow lanes, stopping now and then to see more spices or fruits till we turn a hairpin bend right and Simon points out the local kindergarten. At the doorway two small children were waving, holding the legs of women dressed in brightly coloured saris for safety and security. The women wave and smile and beckon us to join them.

The kindergarten school is a small square concrete structure with three steps from a dusty path that leads into an open room. Quickly ruby-red plastic chairs arrive from nowhere. They give the invitation to sit like royal guests as the children sing songs for us, acting out the stories with hand and eye gestures. It is magical and sweet how excited they are to see us. Lesson plans hang on the walls; today's curriculum is agriculture. Now it's time for photos. Suddenly, two deep brown eyes coming through the door are wide open in amazement! A little girl arrives late for class and running through the door for her lessons today she finds these two white people sitting front and centre in her classroom!

Fishing is the mainstay of the local economy here, easily seen by the many 'Chinese fishing nets' along the edge of the water. It's an impressive but simple piece of engineering that by using balanced weights lowers a net attached to a large steel structure into the water. Lights at night attract the fish to the nets, but they fish during the day as well.

We pull up at the side of the road and Simon leads us down a narrow rubbish-strewn alleyway, past a concrete shack, half-built, where a wood fire is smoking with lunch cooking in a steel pot on top of the embers. Rusty corrugated iron juts out from a hut where a chained black Labrador is eyeing us carefully and silently.

Ahead of us stretches a sizeable Chinese fishing net, reached only by an unstable bridge made from three bamboo planks. It may as well be one. In the universal language of 'I wouldn't if I was you,' the fishermen motion to only step on the middle one. A simple coconut string was all the handhold available to 'walk the plank.' No health and safety here.

Three weather worn fishermen welcome us openly. They show how rocks tied at different heights help to pull up the net. Two times they drop the nets. No fish. Proudly they show a large fish caught earlier that day and feed a net submerged with 'tiddlers' they are fattening up. We gingerly step back to dry land. This 'stopping point' certainly wasn't where the tour would usually go for sure. So there weren't any tourists, only rosebuds.

We head to the local wholesale market district. Entering the busy street full of shouting voices and horn blaring tuk-tuks, a fishmonger selling his wares beckons us over. Soon I'm behind the counter and photos are requested – from him and not me.

There is no disguising the pungent, overpowering stench. Fish, crabs, shrimps, and tiger prawns the size I've never seen are sitting on the ice – their eyes as curious as the schoolgirls at these strange people looking at them. The fishmonger pulls my arm towards a gap in the tarpaulin that serves as the walls. Behind it is a scaffolding structure high above one of the canals filled with litter that are everywhere here. He pulls on a yellow string. The fish that has the other end of the rope tied to its mouth breaks the surface; it must be 3 foot long. The fishmonger explains he is 'keeping it fresh' – I'm not sure but think that is a bit of a misnomer; maybe fresh means something different here.

I ask him about the life he has lived as a fishmonger. He explains that his two daughters will not want to continue what is a third-generation business. 'I understand,' he says to me. 'They want a better life.' His daughters are both training to be nurses and dreaming they could work in England. We chat through the interpreter for a while, and the genuine friendliness of strangers reminds me the world is inherently a good place.

We haven't gone many paces when a regal and stately-looking elderly gentleman calls me into his cattle feed shop. Fascinated I am from England, he wants to practise his English language skills, which amount to telling me he has been to Israel. He pulls from dusty shelves a large notebook. Finding a clean page, he asks for my name and signature. I add a wish for his good health and much happiness too.

Over the narrow busy road I spy a tobacco wholesaler. Like the entrance to an underground cavern, it is dark, with a low ceiling where needles of sunlight are piercing the drapes of dust in the air. There feels a reverence to the room, as if we are entering an inner sanctum. Eyeing us with more suspicion than feels comfortable, hidden in the shadows, a man is counting wads of money. If we were playing a round or two of Monopoly, looking at his hands full of notes, he would certainly be 'the banker.'

Ripping open two small bales of raw tobacco, full of heavy strings of dark brown leaf, they remind me of aged dreadlocks. Simon invites me to smell the long locks of this dark material graded by its strength. He says in hushed tones of English, 'The sales of this "dirty habit" have gone down.' I don't think he realised the man in the corner with the wads of money could speak some English; the speed his smile left and scowl arrived was supersonic. Later, teasing Simon about this, I enacted the scene a few times. He smiled and giggled at the recollection. I enjoy being with him. He opens up his life, telling me stories of his family, but there are threads of sadness and loss woven into the tapestry of his words.

We continue along the busy street overseen by the watching eye of Che Guevara painted high on the walls of a warehouse, a remnant of the rise of communism in the area. The produce market was ending for the day. Heaping bales of bananas onto small trucks, spilling over the sides, wholesale traders headed out. Vegetables of every shape and size have spilt out on to the surrounding floor. Simon's lessons in the variety of produce grown in the area – some I have to say I wouldn't want to have eaten – are told with enjoyment and taste bud memory.

We pass by a narrow shop, squashed between a hardware store and a mobile phone booth. With little room to turn around, customers are entering and others exiting carrying bottles, cans, and containers of all sizes filled with oil crushed from coconuts.

Curious, I peer in and see the shop is the front room of a family home. Family portraits hang from the walls. In black and white images, generations are watching over the trade of this day. The passageway leading off reveals a bed and a small kitchen. It is intriguing to see how 'working from home' takes on new meanings here in Kerala. Simon chats with the proprietor and he enthusiastically invites us around the back of the building to see how this business works.

We enter a time machine.

Rusty machines, generations-old, with crunching and grinding cogs, are working laboriously to crush coconuts to make oil for cosmetics and cooking. It's like watching an elderly man, frail from the years and arthritis paining his knees, struggling with a cane to walk. I ask a few questions and the owner, proud of his antique machines, is telling the same story of a family business, a story that is ending. When he stops working, so will the business that has been in the family for four generations. He is sad but proud. His two sons, their photos on the wall of the mill, are pursuing IT careers rather than the coconut oil business. His sadness expresses deep in more than his words. His sons want to travel to Europe to make their fortunes, then return rich to take care of the family.

In the distance we see a large ornate white church. There are two types of crosses on the churches here – Saint Thomas Cross and Nasrani Sthambams.

It was St Thomas that brought Christianity to this part of India around AD 56. Outside, a large stone Nasrani Sthambams, a giant open-air stone cross, surrounds freshly painted religious statues the height of a small giant. Saints with mournful eyes, baby Jesus held by the Madonna, and monks with brown cassocks. Trying to outdo the church down the street, it seems as if each place of worship competes for the largest gaudily coloured icons and statues they can display outside. I'm not sure what St Thomas might think about it. Parading these statues on top of their buildings, and outside churches in grottos, they look something like an attraction at a theme park or Madame Tussauds waxworks.

Simon leads us around the back of the church compound. There is a substantial sized middle school cohort hanging out of windows and waving. Scores of intrigued young people are watching us walk up the path around the perimeter wall.

A small white single-storey house sits shaded among leafy green trees and bushes. On top of the three steps up to the veranda, a silver-grey haired woman, walking frame held tight in one hand, waves us forward with the other.

In three days, Sarah will be ninety. She is the mother of George, another tour guide and Simon's best friend. Needing to call by and pick up some tour guides to a local monastery George had left with his mom, Simon thought we might like to see inside a typical Keralan home.

Sarah was a teacher and then principal at the school attached to the church for thirty-five years. Her husband, Abraham, passed away many years ago. 'That's his room.' She points to a small side room. I saunter across and see that it has a bed, desk, and shelves full of books, looking much like, I felt, the last time Abraham sat there reading. She invites us into her home.

Dark, cool, and peaceful, faded black and white photos of her parents and grandparents stare back at me as I take in the scene. Religious icons fill the walls, sacred hearts, crosses, and hands clasped in prayer. Contrasting these images is a collection of small plastic sporting trophies. She tells us George's brother, her other son, is a solicitor with six people reporting to him. Proud, she tells us three or four times. It is her grandchildren who have won the sporting awards, we are told. George's children, she tells us again, and again.

Sarah smiles at me as I ask her a few questions about her home and family. We wish her happy birthday and, standing by the doorway, free of the walking aid, she waves goodbye with two hands.

We feel like royalty as the tuk-tuk winds its way through the streets. People wave and smile at us as we go past, excited to receive the same in return, and we realise we have not seen another Westerner all day.

Stopping outside a large factory, and inviting us to take our shoes off, Simon leads us into a large room. Twenty to thirty women are sitting on the floor, hands busy, the volume of the conversation between them filling the air with shrieks of laughter and a bubbling ripple of unknown words.

As we enter, someone turned the volume down. Forty to sixty eyes look curiously at us. They are weaving dried palm leaves into floor mats, coasters, handbags, and trinket boxes. We are visiting a church project that employed women with mental and physical disabilities. It is a day centre of kinds, teaching these beautiful women a skill. It was creating what felt a wonderful sense of community as they sat together. They sell the handicrafts at local markets and send them further across the state. We get the royal tour. Then the sales pitch. But we don't mind. We leave with a beautiful handbag for Noreen. Opening the clasp, we see it is full of rosebuds.

We stop at a second factory. I am wondering if this is the normal route or the regular tourist trail. If we stop at a third, I might get suspicious.

Floods devastated Kerala in 2018, the furious monsoon washing away homes and causing irreparable devastation. We cross over labourers who are rebuilding the driveway and into a handloom weaving factory. Simon points to a line a couple of feet from the ceiling that runs around the walls, its sludge brown and thick. It was the height of the flood in this building. It submerged everything beneath the floodwaters.

Two years later and a few of its ancient looms are clattering, repaired enough and able to work again. Others, to my eye, will remain silent forever. Women were operating the looms at speed with expertise, coordinating feet and hand movements with split-second timing. Still able to have conversation above the din of looms, from the finest of cotton thread, a bolt of white cloth is growing so slowly, a line at a time, as they chat together.

I watch an older man squatting in the corner who is transferring cotton onto a bobbin. He is using a hand-driven machine, perhaps more aged than his years. A piece of cardboard operates as a protective glove, preventing friction burns. His job is to supply the team with endless miles of cotton. There was no pressure to buy anything. This company provides many of the school uniforms that the government gives out freely to all children. They also weave the cotton cloth into traditional dhotis that men wear, a white sheet wrapped around and around the waist. Waving goodbye to a room full of dust and smiles, we return to the tour.

The tuk-tuk pulls to a quick stop at the side of the road. Heading down an alley between plastic sheeting to a large open area, we see women with bundles of coconut fibres twisting and pulling them into coil ropes. Bales of this raw material under their arms, they attach a small amount to a fast, spinning hook on the wall. Trudging backwards, they produce a rope of constant thickness. I ask if I can have a go. 'Pull and twist,' says Simon – then, much as Bruce Forsyth would say on the Generation Game, 'And that's all there is to it!' I reached the end of my rope rather quickly.

Choking dust clouds around the tuk-tuk as we park under a giant banyan tree. Its mysterious branches are like stalactites gently stroking and probing the ground. A crash of mopeds are fighting for any shade underneath it. I'm sure it's older than the temple we have come to visit. It is a Hindu temple where people with mental illnesses or families with children who have disabilities, physical or mental, go to pray for healing.

Walking towards the centre of the complex, Simon tells me at the middle of the shrine is a miracle tree. There is a belief if you bang a nail into the tree with your forehead, it brings healing to those in your family who suffer mental illness. Along with this physical sacrifice and offering, you can sit on an enormous set of scales and give your body weight in fruits, vegetables, even gold depending on your wealth. On the wall a large chart gave costs for individual offerings, I think a sort of price list for redemption and forgiveness. I've always believed grace is a free gift of love – here it seems it carries a price.

A deep sadness cloaks over me as we leave the shrine heading back to the car park. Everywhere I look people sit, or supplicate face down on the concrete, waiting, praying, hoping for a miracle. I hope it arrives for them – and soon.

On the floor next to our tuk-tuk sat an old woman. She had arranged a few cards on a filthy sheet spread out in front. Next to them was a small birdcage, a parakeet inside squawking his displeasure. 'Do you want your fortune told?' Simon enquired, explaining if I gave the woman some rupees the parakeet would come out of the cage, walk among the cards and pick one for me, revealing my fortune in the days ahead. Honestly, I was tempted. Not desiring to know my future, but it would have been neat to see the bird do his stuff.

We stop for lunch a cafe bakery somewhere on a busy road. I have no idea where we are, or how far away from the hotel they have taken us. It unnerves me slightly. We are the local spectacle for the day, all eyes on us as the owner leads us through the shop. At the rear of the cafe is a small room with three tables and a few chairs; blinking blue on the wall a neon sign flashes 'air conditioning.' I decline the offer. I would rather we sit on a table in the main restaurant with a local man, who spies me curiously over his samosas.

We resume what we think would have been the original tour squashed into an afternoon session that was an added extra. Usually our tour was three to four hours, but we'd been going much longer than that by the time we were heading towards the old Jewish quarter.

Simon takes us to an unused but fully restored synagogue. The Jewish community had long since departed the area. Following that, we head towards Paliam Palace, a compound that was the home of the Paliathu Achans (Prime Minister to the Kings of Kochi). We are the only people here. We sit in front of a large TV on the wall and watch a film about the history of the place. We wander the empty halls. While interesting to see and hear about the history of the area, how the Romans, Portuguese, then the British came and left their influences on Kerala. Far more interesting were the conversations shared earlier in the day.

Simon asks us if we want to visit another synagogue? But we give it a miss. 'Take us back to hotel,' I say.

We pose in the courtyard for photos with Simon and our driver, who made our day so special. I know our paths will never meet again. Yet none of this day will be irretrievably lost. This story, and the stories he told, will connect us forever. When I return to Kerala again and again in my mind, I will see Simon, hear his soft rippling voice and gentle laughter.

Simon was holding rosebuds in his hands as we said hello that morning, now gathered into mine.

CHAPTER 8

GRANARIES OF THE PAST

YOU MIGHT ASK, 'WHERE do I keep all these rosebuds I've gathered?' Simple; you store them in the 'granaries of your past.'

Let me explain what that means.

The phrase, 'The full granaries of the past,' came back to me in Vienna December 2019, when we were sauntering through the rooms of an old apartment.

Walking Austria's capital feasts your senses. The street level tempts you with constant stops. As incense invokes praise to gods, the inviting aroma from coffee houses offers me the worshipful delights, tasting luscious bitter mouthfuls of its liquid brown treasures. I pay homage to the coffee god every day, where a slug from a silver aluminium can with two words written in red suffices for Noreen. When it comes to coffee, she is an unbeliever. No wonder synonymous with Vienna is its cafe culture. How could you not enjoy a visit to a city where there is no time of day or part of a meal where coffee and cake is not acceptable? Though to utter 'cake,' for the spectacle of sugar mountains behind glass in these temples, is like pointing and saying, 'hole' when looking at the Grand Canyon.

Angular ivory architecture draws your eyes ever upwards to where, obscuring a plain and bright blue sky, are lines of neat spaghetti, the electric cables powering the incessant squealing trams running on parallel rails buried in tarmac as smooth as the runway at Flughafen Wien-Schwechat Airport. Skipping bike lanes, dodging trams, weaving between cars and pedestrians, we arrive outside the doors of an apartment block built in 1903. Four red and white flags, above an ivory porcelain plaque, tell us we are in the right street. Mahogany brown fades to natural oak where millions of hands have pushed open the narrow door before us. Now adding an imperceptible imprint on its wear and tear, and stepping inside, we push scarfs and gloves in pockets glad to be leaving the frost biting wind outside

We climb the flights of stairs in an ornate building, on Mariannengasse, a side street North of the city centre. The mouth-watering aroma of bread from the bakery opposite drifts upwards with us pulling ourselves over well-worn steps with the help of an intricate, ornate ironwork handrail, each individual spindle a unique work of art. The walls had breathed in the history of generations of people once living there, and now were exhaling its memories. One man in particular had lived there, his life and work interesting me for years.

We reached the floor where the small apartment is tucked away in a corner. Pushing open another narrow door, we walked into the former home of neurologist and psychiatrist Viktor Frankl.

Viktor Frankl is one of my favourite authors. The small apartment in Vienna where he lived, and where he wrote many of his famous books, is now a creative museum to his work and philosophies. A couple of tiny rooms holding curious exhibits encourage interaction and reflection in imaginative and unusual ways. Pulling open what resembled a wall cupboard, inside a small model was inviting me to play and discover the truth that human nature is motivated by the search for a life purpose. Locking eye to eye with Frankl as he climbs mountains in his youth, the bookcase under the life-sized poster spills a few volumes of the prolific outpouring of his life. It's quirky, an ingenious use of such a little space. We spent a couple of hours in those compact rooms – I could have stayed days.

No matter how many times I read Man's Search for Meaning, Frankl's famous book about his imprisonment in Auschwitz concentration camp, it fills me with inspiration and hope. It declares to everyone who would read his words, young or old, that it is possible to find meaning in a world where there are often endless reasons to abandon all hope.

Frankl contends it's possible to find meaning in pain, in the randomness of loss. We can find hope in hurt. We can find hope crawling down dark alleyways, those locations in our life where sadness lurks among the shadows of disappointment and anger. Frankl knows by bitter experience even among brokenness, and the broken, yes, even there, you can find a rose growing through cracks in the concrete of suffering. If we chose, we can gather a rosebud or two when we feel anguish and grief. You can find rosebuds anywhere.

It's Frankl who explains we can store rosebuds forever. He says it this way:

"In the past, nothing is irretrievably lost, but rather, on the contrary, everything is irrevocably stored and treasured. To be sure, people tend to see only the stubble fields of transitoriness but overlook and forget the full granaries of the past into which they have brought the harvest of their lives: the deeds done, the loves loved, and last but not least, the sufferings they have gone through with courage and dignity. From this one may see that there is no reason to pity old people. Instead, young people should envy them."

In our youth, the barns are bare, though I do know some young people that have gathered harvests before their time. I also know some older people whose storehouses look like the empty shelves where once stacked toilet paper before the start of a pandemic.

It is the 'three score' (well, almost) years behind me, filling my granaries for the future, storing those gathered rosebuds away and retrieving them whenever I want. You can't do that so much when you are young. You can't look back on early days. It seems like your mind cannot do that. As you get older, the barn door opens from time to time and looking in are all the memories of my past ready for the future. Frankl reminds me nothing of my past is 'irretrievably lost.' Every experience, every event, every twist and turn down sunny lanes and up the dark alleys of life is 'irrevocably stored.' The person I am today, good and not so good, those deeds done, loves loved, and whatever sufferings just or unjust I have experienced have shaped me. The 'me' I am at fifty-nine and three quarters.

What strikes more is how Frankl soothes the sores of facing future shorter years by reminding me of the riches in these 'granaries of the past.' He suggests the young should not pity the old but envy them. So, take that all you twenty- and thirty-year-olds still wet behind the ears of life. You Gen@ or Millennials, Generation X Y Z, Hipsters, Eboys, and Egirls, and every other subculture that makes up this beautiful multilayered kaleidoscope of life on planet Earth. Go on, I say, envy us 'oldies!' While we may not have the possibility of endless years ahead (but life guarantees no one those) what we have are the 'realities of the past' – the rosebuds we have collected so far stored secure for the future.

Helen Keller says all of life is, 'A daring adventure or nothing.' The days of my life have been rich with so many 'daring adventures.' I may not be wealthy, but when it comes to rosebuds, I'm prosperous. It's something I'm understanding more, getting older, the extent of my vast fortune.

What awoke that realisation in me? First, the day I became older than my dad, and second, standing next to over 700 coffins retelling the amount of rosebuds gathered in another's life. Though it started subconsciously, now I choose to create experiences over owning possessions, and take time mining them for memories.

Travel provides me with many 'daring adventures' for gathering rosebuds. I've been fortunate to visit forty-one countries so far. Gratitude has been my constant travel companion. I travel for many reasons. But what often brings me joy on my journey is it never fails to remind me how much I love home.

No matter how old, I don't imagine wanderlust diminishing. Twelve months or so travelling is not only the preserve of youth. The dream of a 'Gap Year' for Noreen and I still lives and breathes. As long as I can, exploring new cities, meeting interesting people, and having 'daring adventures' is my wish and hope.

That's why I'm here in Kerala.

Chapter 9

A Clutch of Travel Rosebuds

'The world is a book and those who do not travel read only one page.' St. Augustine

The experiences of travelling have enriched the journey of my life. I'm grateful for the blessing of having 'read many pages' across the world. Let me tell you of a few. These are a clutch of the travel 'rosebuds' in my life.

Standing on a sand bar 25 miles off the coast of Grand Cayman Islands as swarms of stingrays dance an underwater ballet around our feet. People on the mainland could still hear Noreen squealing that far away.

Surprising my family by turning up on a beach in Maroochydore, Australia when they thought I was on the other side of the world. Seeing the look on their faces finding 'dad' flipping burgers in the middle of nowhere – priceless.

Staying on the tiny island of Ošljak, Croatia, ferried across in the pitch-black of night from the mainland by the owner of the house.

Snorkelling and canoeing costal lagoons and reefs in Rarotonga in the South Pacific Cook Islands.

Walking the Camino Portuguese from Porto in Portugal to Santiago de Compostela, Spain with my children Laura and Sam. Precious memories.

On a 'Dad and Son' trip to Las Vegas with Sam, riding down the Strip in a stretch limo and taking a helicopter over, and landing in, the Grand Canyon. Unforgettable.

Walking along the 800km Camino Frances (or the French Way) from Saint-Jean-Pied-de-Port in France to Santiago de Compostela in Spain with my 'Camino Buddy,' Larry. More rosebuds per mile than blisters ... well, almost.

Trekking a section of the Annapurna Circuit in Nepal with Gurkha porters and guides. Wandering through mists of incense among temples and stupas in Durbar Square, Kathmandu. Knee-deep in a fast-flowing river bathing an elephant in Chitwan National Park.

Sledging frozen Lake Inari, Northern Lapland, way beyond the Artic Circle being pulled along by a team of husky dogs for three days and nights. Getting dragged face first in the snow, clinging on to the footplate of the rear ice break by my fingertips, was not part of the plan – but it happened.

I hold the world record for the shortest sit on a concrete step in Kotiharjun, the oldest wood fired sauna in Helsinki. Opening the door, I experienced the setting for Dante's poem, The Inferno, while laughing locals poured ever more water on the burners.

Deciding a trip to Istanbul could not be complete without a traditional Turkish bath and massage at one of the oldest steam baths in the city – Cemberlitas Hamami. Then, when seeing the size of the male attendant allocated to me, realising it might not be such a good idea

Watching the sun rise over the ancient fortress of Masada, Israel, the Dead Sea in the distance. Feeling the hairs on the back of neck rise as, unexpected, hundreds of Israeli army recruits finishing basic training marched over the summit at dawn. You could hear their battle cry ahead of them as they came to swear their oath of allegiance never to let Masada fall again – terrifying.

Posting prayers in the cracks of the Western Wall or 'Wailing Wall' in Jerusalem, walking in the steps of Jesus at Galilee, Gethsemane and speaking on the Mount of Olives where the Gospels recount that Jesus ascended into heaven.

Flying in formation side by side with Noreen feeling the G-force pressing our 'Biggles Goggles' ever tighter while looping the loop in a pair of Gypsy Moth open cockpit planes over Lake

Wānaka, New Zealand, then landing by helicopter in the snow towards the summit of Mount Manakau after whale watching at Kaikoura.

Just about making the Trans-Siberian Railway carriage with seconds to spare, traveling two-and-a-half days from Yekaterinburg to Moscow with my interpreter and friend Oleg. Being told to 'shush' for talking by a fierce-faced Red Army soldier standing guard in Lenin's tomb in Red Square, Moscow. I didn't argue.

Trekking Noreen up Lion's Head, the pointy mountain next to the Table Mountain, Cape Town, South Africa, and forgetting to tell her we were paragliding back down.

Staying with a family of Hmong hill people in Sa Pa, Vietnam, and having to play 'Mom and Dad' to a group of backpackers drunk on rice wine.

Chapter 10

Stranger Things

At the end of a bridle path near where I live there is a particular patch of ground which is a bit of heaven. It's about 25 minutes' walk from home – perfect for the outward dog walk on a morning. It's Pete and Pippa's spot. It is also my 'thin place.' A Celtic Christian term for those places where the distance between heaven and earth seems closer somehow. It's hard to explain in words when language doesn't have the capacity to speak what it feels, so silence is a better choice. Rosebuds can be like that too – an experience soaked in mystery, not mystical, or religious, but certainly spiritual, which smacks you into silence. Then awakes within a sense of the divine.

No matter how wet the path gets, this patch is always solid enough for the three legs of my camping chair to stand firmly. We've watched the seasons change here many times. I take a flask of coffee, and Pippa waits expectantly for the gravy bone dog biscuits she knows are in my pocket. I see a sunrise begin over fields and it feeds my soul. There are always rosebuds waiting for me there. They never run out. It's interesting pondering this reality. In dog years, Pippa, my Golden Retriever, is somewhere between her fifty-ninth and sixtieth birthday.

I'm waking up to this morning watching the Periyar River drift by. I could make this spot 'a bit of heaven' number two. However beautiful the moment is, (and it's very beautiful) I am convinced morning coffee is always better shared with a dog.

A call to prayer from the mosque opposite behind tall coconut palms, mixes with caws, hoots, and throbs from unfamiliar birdsong, the enchanting combined chorus drifting towards me across the river. All faiths seem to coexist here openly and with acceptance, a synthesis of religions. That, perhaps, is the way it should be the world over. The coffee is excellent. The morning is magical. I'm feeling it's a good day ahead for gathering.

After a breakfast of eggs, more coffee, and watermelon for Noreen, we do our final packing ready to move on. The hotel staff help to load the cases into the taxi they have arranged. Like the Robert Frost poem, The Road Not Taken, reminds we come this way once, or as Heraclitus supposedly said, 'You cannot step into the same river twice, for other waters are continually flowing on.' I doubt if we will ever return, but if we did, this 'bit of heaven,' this 'thin place' would be somewhere we would return for sure.

If driving is a scary experience in India, being a passenger is degrees higher. Though not speeding around the lanes, the compact car seems to get smaller, shrinking to fit between the local bus heading towards us as the taxi somehow squeezes into the gap of another tuk-tuk he is slowly trying to overtake. He gets so close to a moped carrying a family of three ahead of us. Dad wears a full-face crash helmet, and between mom, who is sitting sidesaddle, a tiny child stands up on the seat, both helmetless.

Glimpses of rural India pass by. Teak logs, trees hundreds of years old by the size of them, are stacked haphazardly in wood yards sandwiched between a mobile phone kiosk and motorcycle repair shop spilling onto the tarmac. The vibrant colours of saris worn by three women, each carrying an umbrella just as bright catch Noreen's eye. They are stark contrasts to grey dust fields of rubbish along the roadside. Local buses have no windows. They fill them to overcapacity, not stopping, only slowing mid-traffic enough for even more people to swell the crowds inside and hanging on the outside. They add home-made stabilisers to mopeds, turning them into trikes on which overweight women swathed in miles of multicoloured cotton carry shopping bags loaded to overcapacity. The same as buses, it appears you can never stop filling them. Roadside stands are selling every fruit, vegetable, and food available. Stopping in the flow of busy traffic, I see a young boy dusting flies off fish for sale part cooking in the sun, which now is hot and high in the sky.

We reach Cochin, welcomed into the city by bridges that span the backwaters, which in a few days we will cruise in a houseboat. Our driver forces his way forward, overtaking where there is no space to overtake and shoehorning his way back again into the flow of the city traffic. Queues build towards a construction site where six men are watching one man dig a hole. Perhaps some things are the same the world over. Trucks carrying bananas stacked high vie for positions with an endless sea of yellow and black tuk-tuks. In the back of an open bed truck, happy young men are carrying festival decorations. They are raucous, singing and chanting – the party looks like it has started already. Replacing my early morning chorus of prayer and birdsong so gentle, the cacophony of car horns never ceases. Eventually, we head out into the countryside, and here the volume of the traffic is less, the sound of horns quieter – not absent – but the driving feels no slower or safer. Rural scenes through car windows are becoming more familiar now. An odd smudged white cow tied to a tree, an egret, his companion not far away.

We are heading towards a village homestay. Google is shouting the directions at us in English. We take ever more narrow lanes, twisting and turning until Google says 'turn left' and we do as we are told making our way along a track which opens up towards a large and impressive house.

Stepping through the elaborate gatehouse is like being threaded through the eye of a human size needle by its shape, and we enter a swept sand courtyard. Stiff legs from the long drive drag, our footprints spoiling the perfection. A mango tree's heavy branches are being supported by wooden scaffold poles. Its branches and leaves offer little shade from the sun as we arrive at our location for the next two nights.

Climbing eight stone steps, two polished golden lions are guarding the entrance to a veranda that stretches the width of the house. Among ancient rattan chairs, teak tables inlaid with glass, and many antiques making it feel as if you are entering a museum, rose a young man, John, walking to greet us. We later learn that it was John's great-great-grandfather who built the impressive house. John's slightly clipped British accent betrays the story he tells of spending his childhood and youth living in the South of England. When his father retired, the family returned to their ancestral home in the village.

John's family traces their history back to the 1770s when, by force, they had to leave the North of the region and came to the village with little or nothing in the way of possessions. Over the preceding generations, they became a powerful and influential landowning family. Farming coconuts gave them a presence and influence, owning vast acres of land in the area. Sizeable, and standing centre of it all, is the magnificent 100-year-old house.

We stand to have our portrait photo taken for local homestay rules and our passports handed over, for which John politely and profusely apologises. He offers us tall glasses of cold, sweet lime ginger soda. Gracefully gliding through the open doors of yet unseen rooms, a petite, silver-haired, immaculately dressed woman joins us, greeting us enthusiastically. It is Rupasi, John's mother.

Though short in stature, Rupasi instantly evokes that she is a woman of substance. Graceful and gentle, the hardly discernible lines on her face betray narratives of loss and sadness, but perhaps power and privilege just as much. As time passes here, we see how many people in the surrounding village defer to her, showing respect to one who holds sway and influence, just as much as an opportunity for work and money. Rupasi speaks with a beautiful lilt to her voice, silk-soft, a blend of upper-class British and Indian. She wants to talk, and I'm fascinated to hear what she has to say. She interrupts John, who is showing us where we can walk in the area on a photocopied map, and he pauses for the moments we talk, but soon he is showing us to our room.

We stumble in shadowy darkness. The corridor is a sharp contrast to the sunlit veranda. Pulling back old brass locks, John reveals the 'rice store' where they gathered the harvest and stored the sacks of rice, a room which is at the heart of any traditional planters' home. Our room for the next two nights is a large bedroom on the ground floor next to the rice store.

Sparsely furnished, decorating the large bedroom with even more antiques, there is a hushed silence and calmness about the room, inviting us to rest. Central and standing proud is a four-poster bed which at mattress height almost reaches my waist. Later we see another bed, even taller, needing steps to climb into so high was it off the floor. With the recent addition of air-conditioning units, the room has modern amenities, and an enormous bathroom through a corridor reached by stepping over significant stone thresholds. It feels impolite to walk on the ruby-red gloss floor imprinted with symbolic gold leaf designs. Through another door with locks the size of a castle's keep, John shows us the black stone seating area, serene, private, and cool. It is here we notice for the first time the overwhelming birdsong that once acknowledged seems to provide a constant communication with nature in this peaceful place.

Lunch is ready, and we follow John through the house to the dining room. The long teak table is full of exotic looking and smelling dishes. On bench seats, on either side, sit Rupasi and the only other guests, Paul and Angela. They become excellent company over the next two days and made the stay here memorable.

Paul is tall, reserved, but not shy. He has a quick sense of humour and a comfortable to be around, laid-back personality. Angela speaks continuously, animating her stream of words with a collection of facial expressions and hand gestures. She is funny, cheeky, a bit near the knuckle, not crude but says the things people often think but don't say. Angela goes in feet first. I warm to her immediately.

Angela's phone never left her fingers, taking videos, snapping pictures, showing scenes from their lives. Angela tells us without asking most of their life story illustrated by photos and videos. 'Alexa, turn on the floodlights,' she says. Back at home, halogen lights illuminate the garden and we see ducks, geese, and chicken coops filling the screen. I spy a couple of impressive classic cars. Angela loves the animals, Paul loves his classic cars.

We enjoy chatting and eating lunch together. The food mostly contains coconut, harvesting a crop from the farm. Savoury but not too spicy curries, rice, and vegetables all grown on their land make for a simple but tasty meal. Over the next two days we will eat well. It becomes a joke as we point out the many ways of cooking the coconut we have at every meal.

Unpacked, we head out for a walk to explore the area, passing Paul and Angela being handed bikes from the man who seems to do everything here. I ask his name, and sadly, I can't quite distinguish what he says through the whispered tones of his voice. He smiles, waggles his head and waves as we walk out the gate and around the lane.

This is rural Kerala. Small shacks covered in tarpaulin and plastic sheeting are the homes where curious locals wave and say 'Hi' as we walk past. The backwaters border the area. Large lagoons are rice paddies, fish farms, and irrigation channels surrounding us on both sides. There are 'Small but beautiful' houses, also 'Large and gaudy' just as much. Paul and Angela ride past, saying that they have seen the North Jetty (we are at the South.) Speeding past their enthusiastically fading voices are shouting, 'The lanes are full of goats!' They ride off in the distance, and we head back to the house.

Rupasi tells us over dinner we could visit a religious festival in the village where the local community is celebrating and worshipping their Snake God later that evening. 'Count us in,' I say, wondering what I might add to my gathered collection for the day.

Cramming the five adults in one tiny car, the man who handled the bikes out is now our driver. He takes us to the shrine of the Snake God about a mile away. The four tourists are somehow in the backseat – how I don't know. While dressed in a beautiful sari, white, trimmed with turquoise blue, Rupasi sits in the front. Her hair is oiled and styled. It is obvious she carries authority and position with ease.

Like sardines, we squash close for five minutes. We could have walked quicker, but I'm guessing that Rupasi doesn't walk lanes often. White fluorescent tubes are hanging from trees, lighting the path leading away from the car. Peeling ourselves out of the backseats, there is an audible corking popping plop as we become ambushed. A crowd of excited boys are demanding water and photos, armed only with smiles. Noreen and I head after Rupasi, who is ignoring the crowd and gliding down a sandy alley lit with more bright pink fluorescent tubes this time. Paul and Angela hang back, mobbed with interest by the children. I'm guessing their photos now being taken by Angela.

Stumbling between a few broken-down buildings, we head towards mystical music playing through a PA system at full volume. There is no space to stand among the crowds gathered. We find the only gap we can, our ears next to the speakers, the vibration of the music echoing through our feet. Not surprising, then, it was the only place empty.

We cannot wear shoes in the temple area. Not willing to remove ours, unsure what we would be treading on, we are spectating the rituals from a distance. In front of the temple, stretched over a large steel frame the size of a sizeable marquee, is a plastic tarpaulin. Beneath are dangling flashing lights and gold tinsel. Covering the entire floor underneath is an intricate design made with vibrant blue, pink, gold, green, and red paint powder. It stretches away from us as bare-chested priests, bright yellow lungis covering dark brown skin, march up and down looking severe.

Lined up just beyond the work of art on the floor, opposite to us, seven young women, varying in ages, but from early teens to twenties at a guess, group together. A priest approaches one girl. Wrapping a red cloth around her head, he marches her backwards and forwards around the painting on the floor. He appears to be trying to induce her into a state of trancelike devotion. Other young women are already giddy with spiritual fervour. Some in the group are rotating, swooning, dancing, and widely waving their arms. Another priest is dousing them with buckets of cold water. I watch this spectacle take place, inquisitive, but feeling a growing unsettlement at the same time.

It is wrong to be critical of what happened next. I do not understand the culture, context, or devotion of the practices witnessed. The priest led a young woman around the paint square. Not easily being induced into a trance by the rite as much as others, marching her around again and again, until she became visibly distressed. It felt more coercion than inducement. We had seen enough. We didn't want to see anymore. We couldn't change the situation so we did the only thing that what we could do – we left.

As we reached the roadside, the man who drove us to the temple arrived with five plastic chairs in the back of the car. Rupasi was standing, and that didn't seem to be acceptable to anyone there. Kindly, he'd brought chairs for the visiting guests as well. Seeing us walking away, he offered us a lift back to the homestay. Arriving safe, in hindsight, best we hadn't tried to walk the dark lanes.

Reflecting on this experience, I am glad we went to see what happens in rural Indian village life. Faith, whatever your particular devotion, is a personal and private choice. Some evangelical dogma I once held tight now sits a bit looser in my hands. Perhaps, in searching out new rosebuds, you gain a changing perspective on previous ones?

Faith, all faiths, fascinate me. I still believe there is more to life than we can see, touch, and feel. The spiritual fervour I witnessed was none more unsettling than visiting some Pentecostal meetings of my youth. Some of those 'receiving meetings,' 'ministry times,' and seeing people 'slain in the spirit' or speaking in tongues seemed at one time valid, if not mystical, spiritual somehow. Then it was something I accepted as a valid religious practice, even took part in. Now I'm not sure about the validity of these religious practices. Who am I to comment on what happened in rural Kerala? But we could choose to not watch – and that's the freedom of choice we took.

The day ended with Paul, Angela, and Rupasi arriving back telling us of what later took place at the ceremony, and how they interpreted the story. We listened over beers shared generously, spicy egg curry, Kerala rice, coconut and vegetables accompanying our conversations.

Leaving the ritual, they had visited another temple close by where the following evening a festival to Lord Shiva would be happening. 'There will be elephants there to receive gifts to the gods,' Angela said, excited and certain she wanted to see an elephant. 'I wouldn't mind seeing what happens there,' I enthusiastically offered in reply. 'I'd like to see an elephant as well.'

So, it looks like tomorrow we are off to another festival – elephants and all. And I'm sure there will be a story to tell.

Chapter 11

The Egg & Spoon Race of Life

We all end up as a story someone will tell one day.

Stories capture something in my imagination, and the ones stirring my heart the most are stories of people. Maybe it's why I find my role in writing eulogies so rewarding? I give each a title, and in a way, each eulogy is a mini life story of its own. 'The Gentleman Within,' 'A Friend Who Holds Life Together, and 'From The First Moment,' are some I've written in recent months. As I gravitate closer towards the life milestone of three score and 'then' the question I seem to ask myself is, what is this story I am writing with my life?

What will be the stories my family will tell of me?

No two lives are the same, not even similar. The uniqueness of each human is astounding. We are our own immaculate conception. We won the first race we entered. No matter if I came last in the egg and spoon dash at junior school, I came first in the race for life. I was a winner from the moment born.

Then the clock started to tick. My life as a story began.

We have little control over those childhood stories; we don't even remember most of them, captured as images frozen in time in photos or snippets of video. Those are the stories we remember or the ones that others tell.

We then start writing our own stories. Decisions we make, and decisions made for us, shape the epic narrative of our life. Before we know it, instead of stories going forwards planning the future, making a career, finding somebody to love who loves us, and perhaps building a family, we start telling stories from the perspective looking back on what happened.

Stories looking forward have no rush; there seems so much time to tell them. Stories looking back need reading as fast as the terms and conditions on a finance deal at the end of an advert for credit on the local radio station, the way they condense 30 seconds of terms and conditions into 10 seconds of garble.

Then one day, before you know it, someone compresses all of a life into a eulogy. That is what I do. I try to capture the essence of a life into twenty minutes. Years into words. Decades into minutes.

It is important to me to continue to hone the craft of writing and be a storyteller of lives. It matters deeply to me. I want those stories I tell of others' lives to be memorable, authentic, and meaningful. Sometimes, honestly, those stories are hard to find. Some lives don't appear to have many stories. The granaries seem empty, an odd rosebud here and there. Hope and future stolen somehow, sometimes, and 'life' just happened. It makes me sad when I am scratching in the biscuit tin of a life for the crumbs of a story.

It's not lost on me, someday, someone is going to do that for my life. My life is full of stories. Stories of adventures, loss, regret, and sadness. Tales of laughter, happiness, and the beauty of being unconditionally loved. I want those stories to last beyond my years.

But here is the rub.

While I want to write those stories with my life, and create memories that will last beyond my life, I'll never know if I was successful in that endeavour. That is why I am writing this story of what happened in between my fifty-ninth and sixtieth birthdays.

This is my story about gathering rosebuds in Kerala. But also the life stories of other people. The people I met, the places visited – intertwined life stories. How my life story during my fifty-ninth and sixtieth birthday and the life stories of strangers in another country will connect forever.

Each life is a story being written. There are rosebuds stored in the granaries of our pasts, however few. Everyone can open the barn door of the past, peering in with wonder at the beauty of recollection. And, while we still have breath, with intentionality, we can go gathering rosebuds in the future.

'Time' is going to continue to fly. It is moving irreversibly forward whether I take advantage of it or not. When I look back on these days from a point in the future, it will be the choices I made today that will lead to telling the story of my life. Will it be a life worth writing about should someone else choose to do that writing?

As we all end up as stories anyway, I want my life to be a good read!

Chapter 12

A Changed Perspective of Time

Question: Today is Monday. We agreed to meet each other on Friday. I call you and say, 'Sorry, I can't make that time, can you put it back two days?' When would we be meeting, Wednesday or Sunday? It depends where I see myself in time.

I hated these type of questions when I was at school. You know the sort – a train is travelling North at 33 miles an hour, with enough coal for 45 miles. The driver is wearing a green overall, has had two cups of tea, and his wife packed him two ham sandwiches. Should he eat one before the train runs out of coal or wait and eat two while they restock the coal? (The answer is at the back of the book.)

Where do I see time? Is time moving forward or me?

The Western view of time is linear, progressing relentlessly forward year up on year. Looking into my life, however positive a spin I put on it, leaves me then seeing my future getting shorter. But what if I switched the way I see time? What if I started viewing the future as behind me, unseen, its length unknown and unimportant, and it's the beautiful vista of the past stretching out in front before my eyes? Could it change my perspective of ageing?

The fascinating truth is some cultures and regions in the world still see time that way. For example, the languages of the Austronesian-speaking people locate the past in front and ahead, whereas the future is behind following on. So, it seems, do other cultures around the world.

Inhabiting the highest Andean hills of Northern Chile are an indigenous people of the Americas called the Aymara. Laura Spinney, a journalist for The Guardian in an article called How Time Flies, writes about an anthropologist from the University of Florida, Marta Hardman, who has been studying the Aymara peoples for 50 years. Hardman discovered something unique about how they speak of time. It is the mirror opposite of a Western view of time. For the Aymara, it seems it's the same – the past is in front of them, the future behind. We see time flowing from a point in front of us through today, our present, and goes back into our past. The Aymara understand time is flowing in the opposite direction – that they have their faces to the past and their backs to the future.

I'm going to call this the rosebud perspective of life.

The idea of walking forward to my past is appealing. The perspective of time living life with my back to the future is worth considering. It's looking through open barn doors into the granaries of my past every day. Life feels richer to me with this perspective because there is so much more of it the older I get. My perspective of life is enlarging each day and not contracting. Getting bigger, not smaller.

The Tongan and Fijian author, academic, and anthropologist Epeli Hau'ofa sums this up perfectly, reminding me – 'we are our history.' I am 'my history.'

'That the past is ahead, in front of us, is a conception of time that helps us retain our memories and to be aware of its presents. What is behind us [the future] cannot be seen and is liable to be forgotten readily. What is ahead of us [the past] cannot be forgotten so readily or ignored, for it is in front of our minds' eyes, always reminding us of its presence. The past is alive in us, so in more than a metaphorical sense the dead are alive – we are our history.'

The past is alive in me. I love that. Coursing through my veins is the lifeblood of being, of existing – all those memories, my collection of rosebuds so far stretching out there before me. Now instead of thinking about the glass of my life being half-full or half-empty, it's the granaries of the past I'm wondering if I can fill up some more? How many more rosebuds can I fill it with?

Somewhere over fifty-nine and getting closer to sixty, I'm caught sandwiched in the present between those two crusts of life – the realities and riches of the past and the potentiality of my tomorrows. Should my years end sooner that I would hope, it's OK. With my perspective of looking forwards and backwards (if you can do that in the next life, whatever that is) I can view it all with gratefulness and thankfulness for my life. The deeds done, the loves loved, and whatever sufferings came my way, I hope I showed courage and dignity through them. And, as Frankl would encourage me, to search and discover meaning even in those sufferings that came my way.

Over my life there is the kindness, generosity, and thoughtfulness I've given, but just as much my faults and forgiveness I required and the grace I've received. I already have granaries full of rosebuds. Yet, if they butter the bread of my life on both sides, and should the future years keep unfolding, there is no reason giving up on the adventure of life. I want to keep ploughing the fields of adventures, to harvest even more memories and safely deliver and deposit these memories – these 'rosebuds' – in the granaries of my past.

It's all a matter of perspective.

Chapter 13

The Lie

Palm trees are swaying gentle in warm breezes, smiling faced children running around our feet, the smell of curry in the air. I'm waking through a small village in rural Kerala when suddenly out from the bushes comes a dog the size of a donkey, foamy froth from its jaws all over my leg where it savaged me. Now I'm in a hospital bed, the same foamy froth on my lips as I try to savage the doctor. I've got rabies!

Then I wake up.

Should we get a vaccine for rabies or not? Seems a simple question, but it occupied my thoughts and dreams and stuck there like a fishbone in my throat for weeks.

Let me explain. I don't do doctors, hospitals, or clinics.

The aversion to being prodded, probed, and pricked with sharp instruments is as deep-seated as the armchairs in the First-Class Cabin on an Emirates flight to India – so I am told. I suffer with S.A.S – 'Surgicaliosis Auto-feinting Syndrome.' Though every doctor, nurse, and A & E porter would deny its existence or validity, as far as I am concerned I've got it – and got it bad.

The sight of a medical instrument or smell of any hospital establishment affects my balance. Gravity increases, rendering me from sitting or standing to lying (usually face planted down to the ground) within seconds. This is not something new. I have suffered with it for years.

When a doctor was drawing out on paper the procedure for a vasectomy, I face-planted myself on the floor before he had even got to drawing the 'cutting' part. Noreen tells me it is true, because I have no recollection of the moment at all. Apparently, so gently it was almost in slow motion, I began rocking backwards and forwards till the inertia heading forward took me from the chair and, with the grace of a hippopotamus doing ballet, I slid from the chair, scraping my head first against the corner desk then proceeding down the doctor's left leg until, face first, I was in a kneeling position at his feet. He turned me over onto my back on the floor. I stayed there prostrate while he showed me the 'cutting' images, looking down from his chair to the floor.

S.A.S. starts in my toes. As it rises upwards, the feeling flushes me hot and cold; I get a metallic taste in my mouth like sucking on a bag of ball bearing gobstoppers. By then I know I need to move, and move in a flash. I need to move my head from its position somewhere above my shoulders and get it in between my knees as quick as I can. As I get older (fifty-nine and three quarters) it's getting harder to assume that position!

It's not dissimilar to an Indian uttanasana yoga position, apparently. It takes devotees years of bending and twisting to get there. I can get into pose in seconds when I see a hypodermic needle. It's not I'm a supple contortionist – I'm about as far as possible from that if the truth be told – but I've been able to manoeuvre myself into that reversed foetal position in doctors' waiting rooms, antenatal clinics, dentists, even once at a chiropodist. I have got into position in three-piece suits just as much as in casual workout gear. Worth saying here, I have little of a collection of workout gear, but you know what I mean. If I don't move quick, it's lights out.

Despite the possibility of S.A.S, my dream of seeing India was too real, too close. The decision is made – we were going to treat ourselves to a course of rabies jabs.

'Where are you heading?' asked the travel nurse at the doctors. 'India,' I reply. 'Oh, you certainly need vaccinations for there,' she says, almost too pleased for my liking. My toes begin the inevitable temperature change from warm to cool and back as the nurse checks the list on her computer screen for India. She's kindly compiling, listing, and telling us about the endless combination of deadly diseases on offer to tourists for free in Kerala. For someone who believes the quick on his little finger is going to turn gangrenous by the end of the week, it's unsettling. I can't pronounce most of the illnesses and conditions on offer, let alone think about even getting them.

I have reordered the worry in my head multitudes of times. I know what's coming next. She will find an illness on the list we haven't already had an injection to avoid. Then she will tell me 'The Lie' – they all tell you 'The Lie.'

With a smile on her face she says, 'You need an injection for typhoid and think about a course of rabies jabs. I can give you the typhoid vaccine now.' Oh joy, thanks. S.A.S is at my knees now and rising supersonic up my legs. The colour of ruddy pink in my cheeks drains to the grey a pair of white underpants get after 12 months wear and washing.

Noreen asks, 'You OK?' She knows Surgicaliosis can strike quick. I have to turn away and look in the opposite direction to my arm where now the sleeve is rolled up. On goes the rubber band, and then comes 'The Lie' – 'Just a sharp scratch,' she says. No! It's not 'just' and it's not a 'scratch,' it's a 'poke in!'

It's in and out, and I am grateful to be upright. I hold on to the cotton wool ball without looking in its direction. 'You might get rabies injections for India just as a precaution,' she says. 'It's a series of three of four injections over a month, but you will need to pay for that. This "sharp scratch" is free.'

She didn't use the term 'sharp scratch,' but I knew that was what she meant. 'Is it necessary?' I ask. 'It's up to you. But get a nibble from a tail wagging mutt with what looks like toothpaste around his teeth and you are a goner.' I think she might have used different medical terms; I can't remember because the feeling that had subsided back to my knees was rising quick.

In the fourteen days following, I lay awake at night dreaming of frothy mouthed dogs and dashes to clinics. There is little risk. So is there little availability of an antidote. Just my luck – there was a worldwide shortage of the human rabies antidote immunoglobulin.

It took three trips this year (and one next year) to a vaccination clinic, where a pharmacist who was the double of Romesh Ranganathan 'spiked' my arm. Those three rabies injections (and one to look forward to) seemed a painful expense, painful in my arm and wallet. But I am now safe to go to places in the world where a bat, dog, or rabid monkey can bite me.

And yes, Romesh told me 'The Lie' as well.

Chapter 14

Speedy and PJ

IN THE JUNGLES OF Brazil, they brew tea from the leaves of tree vines and call it Ayahuasca. It is a powerful hallucinogenic associated with many trips. And here I don't mean a picnic by the river with scotch eggs, cucumber sandwiches, and pork pies. t's the morning after I drank an Indian 'special brew' last night.

Around the homestay grow spice and fruit trees, and of course coconuts. John took us on a brief tour around part of the grounds, pointing out this bush, that tree, a nut, a berry, and a leaf. Pulling the leaves off one vine, he says, 'We call this sleepy tea.'

Our evening meal could not have been better, the food delicious and the company engaging. When Rupasi asked if we would like to end the meal with 'Sleepy tea,' which many guests told gave them the best sleep they ever had, it seemed a sensible idea to agree to a cup or two. Out came a glass teapot, green twigs and branches protruding from the lid, with a faint lime-coloured brew inside. It had little taste. I downed two enormous cups.

The 100-year-old homestay has no glass in the windows. Iron bars, the thickness of bank vaults, fill the spaces instead. At night, pulling back heavy wood shutters and securely bolting them removes all light, and to act as a barrier for mosquitos we can lower roller blinds. Until recently the only form of keeping the room cool were rotating ceiling fans sounding like a helicopter taking off above you or a swarm of bees about to pounce on you. Recently, the house added AC units to the bedrooms. Between Noreen lowering this AC to 'North Pole' settings (she seems to get hot in flushes now and then these days) and the eerie incessant drone of the fan, I didn't know if I slept well or was on a lonely trek through icy and snowy lands in high winds chased by honey bees. All I know is I didn't wake until almost 9:00 am, which for me is unheard. It was the best sleep I had ever had.

Breakfast comprised of steamed rice flour pancakes. Cooking these small little tasty parcels, they split open, and grated fresh coconut filled the pouch. Pouring fresh coconut milk on the top, and a good glug of honey (the mere mention of the word sending shivers up my spine) over the top, they were delicious.

Conversation was difficult. John explained the headlines of riots taking place in New Delhi. Many were dead. The roots of the angst in the Citizenship Act, causing reverberations across the nation, along with growing concerns about a strange virus spreading out of China and a cruise liner in isolation. A sombre end to our meal.

Rupasi arranged for two tuk-tuks to arrive taking us on a local tour. Hearing the now familiar 'put-put-put' noise of the engine whining up the drive, we head out down eight steps and across a perfectly swept courtyard our feet making tracks in the smooth sand just as we would in untouched snow.

In front of the gatehouse were two three-wheel tuk-tuks. Ours had seats the colour of 'sleepy tea,' which was disconcerting and left me feeling ominous about the day ahead. By the side of our chariots for the day were two smartly dressed drivers, black trousers and tan shirts pressed to perfection.

The older of the two drivers had the most perfectly trimmed moustache I've ever seen. It sat on his upper lip with pride, each whisker as straight as the seam in his trousers. The younger's facial hair was not so neat, but magnificently wild, like a mischievous caterpillar. His black hair was just as rebellious, which I saw him often checking in the mirrors. I noticed on the side of his tuk-tuk a silhouette of Elvis Presley. Raised in the air, his hand is like the iconic pose singing 'The Wonder of You.' I say, pointing at the large sticker, 'You like Elvis?' The young driver looks at me weird and animatedly says, 'PJ, PJ, is PJ!' So it stuck.

We climb in behind our driver, and Paul and Angela offered to follow behind with PJ. PJ took off like a rocket. We saunter along 200 metres behind, flat-out. I could have walked quicker than 'Speedy's' tuk-tuk.

By the time we got to the blue tarpaulin-covered workspace in the woods, Angela had taken seven videos and twenty-six photos. She was 'chatting' animatedly to the group of about twenty women who were peeling shrimps. The speed that they deftly shed the shell of these small crustaceans was incredible. At a few pennies per kilo peeled, no wonder. A quick wash in the bowl, snip, snip, snip, and done.

I chat with a couple of women, Speedy helping me with odd words. Hunched down, her legs thin spindles with swollen knees, looking like a large knot in a piece of rope, one of the women tells me she is 85 and has been a 'peeler' all her working life. The smiles and laughter come easy among the group, I'm sure some at our expense, the workplace obviously a time to chat and gossip amidst never-ending shrimp peeling toil.

There is a younger woman wearing the most amazing earrings looking like mini satellite dishes, almost touching her shoulders. Through the guide, she tells me she likes chocolate. I'm not sure if I hear him right; are the batteries low in my hearing aids, or did she say something else? No, she wanted to let me know she liked chocolate. Repeating this again, the women in the tent like space laugh and giggle. I miss out on the joke, but gain a rosebud or two. We wave goodbye, thanking them as more buckets of unshelled shrimps arrive.

As we drive around, signs are showing communist parties are in local power. I'd like to know more about how could it fit with the caste system?

We stop by a tiny house with a large workshop attached, 'Speedy' beeping his horn. I wish I knew his name. He tells me many times, but sounding eight to ten syllables long I could never repeat it, let alone try to write it. Speedy it will have to be. I like him. He must have done 'the tour' many times before, but he is alert, welcoming us into his world and enjoying his job, which makes the day special for us.

We enter a workshop where coconut doormats are being made. On a vertical loom using steel rods, the weaver soon shows how the mats we have in hardware shops at home are produced. She makes over a hundred a day for £4. Given the speed she worked, and the relentless nature of the job, we find to our surprise it was her day off. We gave her a gift of rupees and the smile said it all; generosity begets generosity.

Our next stop was a Hindu shrine. We pull into the rough square patch of wasteland that served as the car park. Paul and Angela were already out and, with shoes in hand, walking along the covered portico towards the temple. We take off our shoes, but not our once white, now greying socks. Signs everywhere say no photos. I wonder how Angela is going to cope.

The pervading reverence in the air is punctuated by the sickly-sweet redolence of hundreds of burning oil lamps surrounding the structure of the altar. Two teenage boys, bare-chested, in white lungis are beating a rhythm on drums in procession with two ashen-faced priests, dressed in orange and ochre, all parading around the shrine. It was only us six watching. No worshippers. Just the procession of four around and around the shine. It took about five minutes to circumnavigate.

Once was fascinating. Twice was interesting. Thrice the word captured my attention more than seeing them march past four times. I have to say they were giving it everything they had got, banging the drums with as much fervour as Phil Collins playing 'In The Air Tonight.' Seeing enough, I ask Speedy if he knew where we can buy beer.

The previous evening, Paul and Angela had generously shared their Kingfisher beer with us. The rules in Kerala limit buying alcohol to only in local government marketplaces. So, wanting to return their generosity, I hope to buy some beer to share over dinner tonight. Zooming off at the pace of a saunter, and spinning 180 degrees at the rush of a snail, Speedy is taking us to the local beer store.

We park up opposite a dumpsite. Scattered high and deep were cardboard sheets and yellow plastic boxes, bits of broken furniture, and mountains of plastic bottles crushed, the dusty remnants of thirsts quenched now suffocating the earth below. On one pile is a large wooden board where ripped red and yellow political posters are pasted three high by three wide, with one blue plastic flip-flop sandal resting on the face of the prospective candidate. His piercing eyes are looking directly at the worn sole. Well, one eye; the other was looking in the opposite direction, the poster torn. There must be something about a three by three repeating pattern of posters for political parties here. Is this the local tip for past elections? Another wooden board, its nine posters missing most corners, had an intense young man screaming into a microphone – well he once was, now it's more of a whimper into a broken bottle of Kingfisher beer smashed over him. This, strangely, makes me hopeful.

An obviously well-trodden path leads through the middle of the trash and was disappearing around the back of a few ramshackle buildings. An unbroken stream of men was coming and going. It resembled a line of ants tracking a scent across the ground. Joining in with the march, and following the crowds, there was excitement in air. Mostly mine. I followed Speedy while Noreen stuck close to me. We didn't know what was safer, leaving her alone in the tuk-tuk or entering the local Majestic Wine Store. The obvious addition to this line of intrepid explorers in search of alcohol was one white Western woman – it was hard to miss her. Every face coming towards us was open-eyed at the woman passing by in the opposite direction.

We turned the corner around the concrete building to find a small market was taking place. A couple of homemade stalls were selling food bubbling and boiling over, lottery tickets, fruit, and vegetables. Bollywood music is blaring from speakers, and I spy a frantic queuing system in place.

A gaggle of men (and now one Western woman) heading towards the bargain booze store were corralled through a narrow walkway made of a steel cage. It reminded me of the way a farmer herds livestock down an ever-decreasing walkway ready for milking. There was one way in and one way out – a one-way system the width of a slim, Keralan man. Speedy started pushing me forward against the flow of now happy purchasers to enter the fray by going into the 'out' queue. Sensibly, Noreen stood back to watch the show.

On and on he pushed me towards the front of the sales counter as locals with small bottles of rum, brandy, and whiskey were pressing against me the other way. It wasn't long before the inevitable was going to happen. Attempting to squeeze a Western man the width of two medium-sized Keralan men into the caged walkway against the flow of traffic, I caused a blockage in the system that no amount of Mr Muscle would unblock.

Pushing and urging me on ever forwards into the hordes of thirsty drinkers unable to raise a bottle to their lips, Speedy hollers something to the baying throng. I'm guessing it was, 'Look guys, if we don't let the overweight tourist get his beer first, you won't get yours – look, he's now stuck in the cage.' Not with an ounce of reluctance, but genuine openness, like a well-oiled military parade, the crowd reverse marched in step and let me get to the sales counter. It was a steel grille more secure than the local bank. Through a tiny gap I handed 400 rupees – four Kingfisher beers came back. Was that a cheer I heard as we were leaving or the slurp of movement rushing through the vacuum I'd created? No matter – we have beer.

We make two more stops. The first was at a weaving factory where they made enormous floor matting. Three men working one loom in precise coordination wove enormous carpets from coconut fibre string. Hot, dusty, and claustrophobic, these men worked in awful conditions. Bare-chested, thick dust in the air, I don't know how often tourists call by to observe their toils, but they welcomed us, smiled, and waved. This was one activity I would not ask to have a go at.

Our last stop of the day was at a Catholic church dedicated to St Mary. There were similar colossal statues outside the buildings devoted to all the saints, but particularly St Thomas again. Yet this was different. On this site, there were ancient stones purported to be from one of the first churches built in AD 56, when St Thomas came to India from Israel. Like viewing the Crown Jewels in the Tower of London, next was the sight of a holy relic. Set back behind glass and steel bars, elaborately mounted on a gilded frame, was a wooden cross missing one corner. Belonging to St Thomas, the part missing was boiled and used for healing, so the legend told. Paintings depicted its miraculous properties, above which a gaudy pink neon digital clock was telling us it was time to head for home.

Squashed tight into toxic lime-green seats, we zoom off at the pace of slow walk. I'll never know how, the tortoise and hare reenacted, we reach the homestay first. After a photo session together, we wave goodbye to Speedy and PJ. Rosebuds gathered, now tired, the afternoon wiled gently away resting, writing, and snoozing.

It's early evening, before dinner, and we are six up in the compact car again. Tonight we are heading towards to an impressive Hindu temple complex surrounded by a lake. Fireworks light the sky as we arrive, mirrored in rippleless water. Triumphal music blasts out. People shout and sing – there is a party atmosphere in the air. Angela, like an excited child on Christmas morning, spies the elephant at a distance through the car window. We are told to hurry, as it will be his last circuit of the shrine for the night.

Before the car had stopped, I'd removed my shoes. Hundreds of barefoot people are in the complex – and four tourists' pale legs wearing coloured socks covering white feet join them. My socks, once white, are a shade of Keralan grey. Angela's are stripes of royal and pale blue. Two pairs of socks set off in hot pursuit of an elephant.

Angela and I snap photos of the elephant's backside swaying easily from side to side as we run past thousands of oil lamps and overhead exploding fireworks cascade into the night sky. I get three or four shots – she gets a hundred. I don't know what Lord Shiva would have thought as we pass the temple shrine at speed, now overtaking the elephant. We both abandon any sense of reverence for the religious site, racing ahead to see the trunk end of this majestic animal, leaving Noreen, Paul, Rupasi, and our driver in the dust of our dirty socks.

Bedecked in a jewelled trunk shawl, the mahout brought the marvellous matriarch to a stop and climbed down, tying her to a stake in the ground. Small pink ears twitched, and even pinker freckles ran the length of her trunk. Tied around each foot and connecting over her back are heavy steel chains. This makes me sad. What was I expecting? This is a wild animal in captivity serving her masters.

Again, I find I'm struggling with the balance between awe and culture and challenging to reconcile them. This beautiful animal is shackled and in servitude. Earlier in the week on the front page of The India Times, next to a small report of a cruise ship racked with a strange virus, was the story of a temple elephant that had the honorific title of Gajaratnam who had died aged 80. It had served in a temple for 66 years, carrying the thidambu of Lord Srikrishna. Doctors had been watching his health after a week of diarrhoea. (So far, I've had no use for the 12 boxes of Imodium, 2 boxes of rehydration salts and two corks that we packed.) But sadly, the elephant died. The loss seemed significant, the piece filled with a sense of grief pervading the words. A revered animal alive in servitude, sad at its death.

This beautiful elephant before us was now being removed of her ceremonial adornments. Behind her, and shackled much the same, was another elephant who would lead the procession around the shrine much later that evening. This was a male tusker. I know because Angela suggested that if you walked underneath it, you could get knocked out by that thing, pointing somewhere to the back end. We took a few more photos as the rest of our party were now joining us. The elephant mahout gave the universal sign of money (fingers and thumbs rubbing together) to stroke the elephant. We all declined.

Wandering this festival differs from last night. Laughter and squeals can still be heard above the rhythmic sounds of drums beating through speakers high in volume on the tops of poles around the perimeter of the temple. The tension of the previous evening is missing. Children grasp strings on helium balloons or wave neon light sticks as they run with freedom. Groups of families gather, enjoying the evening festivities. There is celebration in the air rather than fear. It feels like a carnival of happiness amid devotion. I curiously watch an offering ceremony taking place in the centre of the shrine. They drizzled a large basket of rice into a brass bucket. At the end, when the bucket was full, money changed hands, saying a prayer, and then the rice went back into the basket, only for the next person in line to repeat the same act. The queue was long, the devotion fervent, the wads of money abundant.

I left the temple with much different feelings than the night before. Though still not understanding everything that happened, here was a sense of happiness and celebration, not a feeling of control and coercion.

I'm almost sure as our group left through the gate and squashed back into the car, I heard peals of laughter and someone saying, 'Running with socks on, they were, running with socks on...'

Chapter 15

Warm Hearts or Warm Blood?

Is youth wasted on the young? The days, as the poet Herrick says, when 'Youth and Blood' are warmer? Are the years of youth better? I'm not necessarily sure they are. Yes, we have the boundless energy and unbridled ignorance of youth we think is self-confidence. Yet, if we reached around and felt the back of our ears, it might surprise us to find a few damp patches are there.

Optimism is bursting out of every pore in our 20s and 30s. So much time ahead. We are invincible. When I was in those years, I was like that. What I didn't realise then, and wish I had, is how quick it would all pass. Get in your 40s and 50s and you feel time is speeding up and running out. I never pictured one day I would be an old man. One day, and soon, I will be in my 60s. There is a gratefulness within, nonetheless, for reaching nearly sixty. The moment I felt the years creeping on me was the day I became older than my dad. He died too young. When I passed the age dad died, it was a significant milestone in my life. I often think about what kind of old man he would have become. He never got old. Dad will forever be in his 40s.

When young we might pass the 'old-aged pensioner,' or other perhaps more derogatory synonym, from down the street, dawdling, getting in our way, never imagining one day young people will look at us and think the same thoughts we used to think. Now, I picture myself as the old man I want to be. I see him each morning. Not in the mirror, but in the park when I am walking the dog early each day.

Short, lean, slightly stooped, he is in his late 70s at a guess, might be early 80s. Though tanned, his bare sinewy legs are uneven in their gait. They still allow him to run about five miles each morning. He is a bit weaselly-looking and still moves as quick. Bright green fluorescent jacket, bobble hat, and shorts. I've followed him setting off up the lane by where I live and watched him return 40 minutes later. That's the old man physically I would like to be. I see other old men, propped up on walking sticks, shuffling along. I hope I don't become that kind of old man. Truth is, I will probably be somewhere between, as I don't run up the lane now!

The physical aspect of old age is worrying, but will fade one day. No matter what I do. What I never want to lose is the burning fire and spirit inside. The awe, splendour, and curiosity for this magnificent thing called life. Is it really possible? Some people believe it is.

The old man I want to be is the kind French psychologist Marie de Hennezel describes in her book – The Warmth of the Heart Prevents Your Body from Rusting. She writes how some people who live the golden age of their lives do it with presence, accepting the inevitability of ageing, but do so without becoming old. It was the title of the book caught my eye first. It's the title of a song centenarians on the island of Okinawa in Japan sing every morning. There are more people there who live to be 100 years old than anywhere else on earth. Their secret is no secret at all – diet and exercise explain some reasons for their long lives. They link critically just as much to a positive state of mind and a well-developed social life, along with daily spiritual practices. So being old is as much a state of mind as it is a physical reality.

As I become older, I want to be someone who radiates joy and happiness regardless of my age and physical capabilities. I don't want to become a 'grumpy old man' complaining about everything happening and how young people don't understand what it was like in our day. I want to be an old man people would enjoy spending time with. Someone who listens to the stories of others' lives rather than boring everyone retelling the stories of my life. I think there is an opportunity to approach ageing as an adventure. Instead of becoming embittered, I want to be interesting and interested – a person attractive to be around. This is the perspective of ageing positive and optimistic – a looking forward to and into the future of my past.

So, I want to clarify that this book is no whinge on lost youth. It is the celebration of a life lived, of pasts remembered, and expecting exciting futures ahead. It's a matter of finding that perspective.

Chapter 16

Thomas Cook, Teletext, Tripadvisor – The Evolution of Travel

We will be travelling to India with the reliable tour company – 'Pete's DIY Tours.'

'Pete's DIY Tours' have been in business for many years. There is as much enjoyment from planning, booking, and researching a trip as experiencing it for me. Well, almost. Our independent travel adventures have taken us across Europe, America, and as far as Vietnam, New Zealand, and the South Pacific, and now they will take us off to India. Or will they? Somehow, those far-off places felt safer to organise a trip. I'm not sure India is any more daunting; perhaps it's the creeping years to old age leaving me more uncertain about organising a trip to India myself?

That's one thing I'm noticing about decisions and choices I'm making getting older. I'm becoming more aware of the steps I take, trying to be sure of my footing. My kids joke about 'Dad has had a fall.' Never Dad 'fell over.' That change of language about old age is subtle and immense at the same time. Is there such a thing as a lexicon for old age? The definition of 'old age' at Dictionary.com is – 'the last period of human life, now often considered being the years after 65.' In that case, at fifty-nine and three quarters, I'm not there yet. The terms second childhood, evening of life, and golden years sound much better and something to look forward towards rather than decrepitude, senility, and geriatric. Even those 'exciting' stages of old age sound better than – deceased.

The wonder of looking through glossy colour magazines for places to visit captivated me for years. Our local high street once consisted mainly of banks, building societies, travel agents, and a new enterprise – charity shops. These days, the way ivy takes over a house if left unchecked, it's mainly charity shops that remain.

The layout of a travel agents was simple. On one side were desks with terminals, behind which sat sales assistants dressed very much as air crew cabin staff. On the opposite side was the mother lode of brochures. 'Can I help you sir?' Would come the question from a blue-suited assistant. They'd probably been pointing, saying to each other, 'He's back again '

I'd side-shuffle down the shop and across the world. First stop, Mediterranean. Think package holidays to Spain and Portugal. Moving further down towards the currency exchange window I would pass North Africa. Think Tunisia, Morocco – Souks and snake charmers. Two racks on was Greece. Think – Shirley Valentine, tavernas, and Acropolis. Then moving across the world and east we would arrive at the Red Sea resorts, Eilat, Taba, and Egypt. Think food poisoning and camels. Though not quite the shortest route to travel overland, the next racks were USA. Think Disney resorts and Las Vegas Baby! Then the Cruises rack would come into view. These were out of reach, and only for the 'oldies' anyway. Who'd want to go on a cruise?

Those were delights I was grateful to experience, but yes, when older.

I could meander in the travel agents for ages. I would arrive at the 'luxury' rack – Audley Travel, Kuoni, Abercrombie and Kent, and Thompson 'Faraway Shores.' Think hammocks swinging from palm trees, Concord flying you supersonic to exotic locations like Hong Kong, African safaris, and the Far East. It was the stuff of travel wanderlust dreams in those days, the names of these tour companies sounding as mysterious as the destinations they visited.

Resources collected, I would head home for operation research, excited in the same way I was each November when the latest Freemans home shopping catalogue would arrive at home. I would sit for hours flicking through the pages. 'I want that, that, that, and that.' Penciling the items ready for my Christmas toy list for Santa.

Dates booked, and destination chosen, my next task was the time-consuming, hair-pulling process of using Teletext.

Teletext was a way for displaying rudimentary text and graphics on an equipped TV. Press the red button on your remote, select Teletext holidays and pages of travel agents would appear. Interesting, in 2020, as I am writing these memories, the demise of Teletext will be for good. Buying flights on Teletext was frustrating. A page of text would show holiday deals, discount prices, and a telephone number. If you missed the page, or didn't get the telephone number down quick enough, you had to wait until page 30/32 clicked around again. I would spend ages finding the same hotel and flights seen in the glossy magazines, and then as many hours bargaining with a person at the end of the phone. But it worked. It opened up travel for us at an affordable price.

Then the internet arrived.

These days, I spend longer on the internet researching where I am going than the time I will be there. I 'fly' over a place with Google Earth. I can walk from the train station in Pisa, Italy to the hotel where I am staying on Google Street View. I know what the route is like. I can 'see' the bus stop where to get on and where to get off. You might think this takes away the mystery? Not at all. I often end up taking routes looking more interesting in the moment I didn't plan. It makes the process of planning trips easier. Just as much, reading the reviews from TripAdvisor and Airbnb take some concerns away for finding places to stay. The internet has made being an independent traveller simple, affordable, and accessible.

The 'India' plan started taking shape. Arriving in Cochin International Airport, we would head towards the coast. Then we would move inland and climb towards the tea plantation of Munnar. Heading across to the wildlife centres of Thekkady and back towards the beaches South of Cochin. We would stay in a mixture of homestays and hotels.

But I couldn't stop this nagging thought pecking away at the back of my mind.

As independent travellers (and fifty-nine and three quarters at that), it's a long way from home with no contacts in India should we have any problems. And after reading the foreign travel advice on government websites, there was plenty of opportunity for those. Death by disease, dangerous driving and riots were top of their list, not quite the sightseeing plans of mine though. With a certain resignation and a feeling of admitting defeat, perhaps now, after years of being an Independent traveller, had the time arrived to employ a travel agent? Was 'Pete's DIY Tours' to be no more?

I found a recommended travel agent who could book everything for me. Not that I needed suggestions or routes, it was more feeling at least I would have a contact in the country of kinds. I sent the agent my 'plan' and he set about confirming bookings direct with the places I wanted to stay. So far so good, but nothing I couldn't and hadn't already done myself. It became confusing for the homestays. Was this the same 'Mr Peter who'd emailed us?' But the agent returned emails quickly, messaged me on WhatsApp and built enough trust to think the idea was sound. He was helpful, filling me with confidence and assurance – until. Until I wanted to pay. He asked me to bring him a bag of United Sates dollars in cash when I arrived in India, promising me he would meet me on my arrival at the airport with tickets and vouchers for the trip.

No. I don't think so.

'Pete's DIY Tours' was back in business.

Chapter 17

Are You with Audley?

IT WAS PITCH-BLACK. THE blinding darkness where you can't see your hand in front of your face dark. My phone lights up the gloom and tells me it's 6:10 a.m. The absence of 'sleepy tea' after last night's coconut-infused dinner means I am wide awake. My body clock now in sync with local time.

Fumbling across the bedroom, the concrete threshold in the doorway reminds my stubbed toes it's there. As usual, my attempts at being quiet in a morning fail miserably. Noreen slumbers on. I'm worried she could have frostbite from the low temperature setting and maximum power on the AC. Clunking, the solid wooden bolts crash back. I pull the door open to the black stone veranda attached to our bedroom. It's as dark outside as inside. I grab a bottle of water, a head torch, and walk around the lightless homestay to the large open veranda at the front of the house to spend some time writing. I set up the iPad and switch on the head torch. Mistake. Within seconds, swarms of critters cluster around the light. There are bottles of DEET spray on the table – now I understand why.

A patch of sky between treetops opposite changes colour – purple, through cobalt-blues, to pinks and oranges. Birds dart. Flickering silhouettes dashing around blacker against these changing hues. Their blackness against the burst of colour imprinting this rosebud moment for ever on the photographic memory of my mind. There is a rush of warm stillness amid the birdsong, a serenity between the caws, hoots and calls, carrying with it the fragrant promise of a new day. A distant flute starts drifting upwards a prayer to the gods, harmonising with the feint buzz of mosquitos. This is a 'my India' moment.

Shocked to see me as I am him, a young man appears out of the darkness of the gardens. This other early riser was there to collect Rupasi's renowned lime and ginger soda mix. Her brother-in-law was hosting a meeting later that day. Without Rupasi's special welcome drink for the guests, he feared it was doomed to failure, hence the frantic early morning dash.

Alone again, I sit in the dark and listen to the choir of mysterious birdsong singing unknown arias. From the temple we visited a couple of days ago, a second flute joins in – a dawn concerto crescendoing a greeting to the sun as it rises into clear blue skies. The housemaid, seeing I was awake, brings me a flask of coffee. Rosebuds and coffee. My dog would have loved this morning.

Noreen and I were expecting another fun breakfast with Paul and Angela. We all move on today. They go to Cochin, heading on towards their journey home, while we are moving up to higher ground and another homestay. After an enjoyable breakfast, including various coconut selections, we head for our taxis.

Saying our goodbyes, we both agreed Paul and Angela were good company. Noreen and I have never been 'holiday friends' sort of people. Other people we know meet a couple on holiday and become lifelong friends. Maybe we have missed an opportunity in the past to enrich our life, and the lives of others? The coincidental and serendipitous meeting of Paul and Angela made the stay here certainly filled with laughter and fun, and made it more memorable. They were great company, and I hope we were just as much. It's fascinating; we travel halfway around the world and meet a couple who live few miles from us, but I don't think we will ever see them again. That's sad in some way. Our lives and our stories are connected forever. I wonder how the elephant story would sound from Angela's telling? For sure, I'm certain it would be accompanied by laughter and hundreds of photos of an elephant's rear end! We wave them down the drive, and onto adventures new. Travel on, travel safe Paul and Angela.

It seems fitting as we leave to pose for a photograph with Rupasi on the grand steps leading down to the gatehouse. She was a woman with substance, like the entrance to the house. Between the spaces in our conversations, she shared life narratives, intriguing me. She was someone with who I could spend hours in conversation and still feel there would be more for her to tell. In the background, on the veranda, John is apologising profusely, but so politely, to a couple newly arrived. 'Would you mind awfully,' he asks, 'to stand so I can take a photo for the homestay rules?' The cycle is unbroken.

We leave, grateful, our arms gathered full, and for this new couple, rosebuds sit around the grounds, on dawn verandas just waiting to be gathered. Will they? If not for these visitors, they will be there for others. Rupasi pushes into Noreen's hand a small gift of an oil lamp to remember our stay. Still, with many beautiful experiences to add to the storehouse of our lives, we will never forget her and here. We can always come back again and visit in our minds.

The road heads inland. The streets are chaotic; no harmonious arias here, more a display of experimental percussion played on scooter horns, Tata engines accompanied by tuk-tuks with asthma coughing and spluttering – deafening and captivating me passing by.

We leave busy towns, now reaching the countryside, our journey climbing ever upwards passing rubber plantations and pineapple fields. I follow the route on Google Maps. It's a habit I keep when travelling overseas on 'Pete's DIY Tours.' I make sure I know where we are and if we are heading in the right direction. I don't know what I would do if I discovered we weren't.

Our taxi driver today must go to the same barbers as PJ. His hair is a work of art, more expressionism than classical. He is polite, helpful, and curious about us as tourists. Avoiding potholes is a skill here and, missing craters big enough to swallow a small child, he turns with care onto a side road. It's so unmade, it's not on the map. There is a slight feeling of uncertainty heading into the unknown. This is our first experience of what will become commonplace in the days to come, underestimating the time it takes to travel from place to place.

The roads in rural Kerala turn from smooth tarmac, runway quality, to a series of potholes in 100 metres and back again. Speed up. Dead slow. Spurt forward. Crawl. Jolting from side to side, a journey of a few miles takes hours. I'm not sure if it is law here, but each taxi driver has some kind of statue on the dashboard, like we would have had a tax disc in the window. The yellow smiley face, like a marble on a pencil, is spring-mounted and waves manically to us in the back as we try to look to the road ahead through the windscreen. Though bone-shaking, stomach-turning and having the capacity to allow me to taste my coconut breakfast a second time, the driving is not erratic. They overtake the car ahead so slowly, and with little haste, no matter a bus is speeding towards a full head-on collision. Negotiating the miles takes skill and endurance to avoid these holes, cars, motorbikes, and trucks streaming at you on the same side of the road. We eventually see a sign directing towards our next stopover. Driving a further kilometre along on a dusty, winding track deep into the countryside, we arrive at our homestay.

Greeting us, a smiling young woman in a beautiful pink sari anoints us with bhasmam, ceremonial ash, and vermilion. By her side were bowls of beautiful purple and yellow blooms, vibrant, and putting the burning sunshine to shame by their radiance. She places garlands of jasmine flowers over our heads, their fragrance filling our room during our stay. Standing behind her was Vichuz, the owner of the homestay. Short and slight in build, he had darting white eyes, scanning us and everything before our leaving the taxi, not missing anything. Sounding a little abrupt, with no hint of a greeting, he says to me, 'You never answered the email I sent.' (I checked. He sent it 30 mins before we arrived.) Polite and condescending, funny and stern, demanding and sociable, helpful and blunt, Vichuz is a mixed bag of contradictions we come to experience over the next two days. I like him immensely.

'We do not allow shoes in the house, you're not in Europe now,' he tells us. Vichuz leads the way to our room on the second floor. We follow barefoot; I'd abandoned socks by now. The homestay is bigger than I imagined from the website. The bedrooms are plain, clean, and spacious. Vichuz points to a pack of information leaflets on the table. My eye catches the phrase in bold on the first sheet, "If you feel at any point of time during your stay that you have come to the wrong place, inform us." Vichuz informs us lunch is finishing – it starts at 1:30 pm, all the other guests are eating, go now and join them. I wonder if I should suggest I'm feeling maybe we are in the wrong place? But decide against it before lunch, as I'm hungry.

Walking into the dining room was like walking into a classroom on your first day of school, except everyone else started the week before. Six Australians are chatting and laughing with two Brits. Four French are deep in conversation between themselves. Between the two groups sit four place settings. We take two next to the Brits. The food arrives, served by young men who over the next two days I watch and admire. They are relentless in their efforts to take care of us, under the ever-watchful eyes of Vichuz. Grown on the homestay, our meal is magnificent. Kingfish, vegetables, and Everest-sized mountains of fluffy white basmati rice. No one at the table raises an eye towards us or acknowledges us even though I smile at the group from Oz. I make eye contact with the Brits and even wave – nothing. Awkward. Hurried, Vichuz arrives with two more guests and sits them opposite to us. Admonishing them for being late, Michael and Hazel look suitably chastised. 'Sit here,' he barks. Vichuz maybe the equivalent of an Indian Basil Fawlty. Are Michael and Hazel wondering if they are in the wrong place too?

'Are you with Audley?' Hazel asks. Audley Travel, so their website says, are experts in tailor-made travel. It sounds so wonderful – and expensive I'm guessing. 'They manage all your reservations and logistics, so you're taken care of from the moment you step off the plane until your return,' she says. I'm taking a guess people who travel with Audley often shop in Waitrose and buy clothes from House of Fraser. Audley adverts appear in upmarket travel magazines and The Times Travel Supplement on a Saturday. If you are in the market for an Audley holiday, undoubtedly, they would care for you well from airport to the hotel and back. Maybe they should have been the tour company I contacted? I'm sure it would have been magnificent – but we are not Audley Travel customers, our budgets are more minimal, so it's 'Pete's DIY Tours' for us.

I don't really know, as I didn't ask the dreaded question, 'So what do you do?' Hazel reminds me of someone who could be the president of her local WI, a retired High Court Judge or similar. Michael reminds me of someone ex-navy, quite happy to go on the long walks he loves alone. We chat with them over lunch politely, listening more than asking questions. They speak quiet, slow, and intentional. It was reassuring we were not invisible. For a while I thought we were in a dream and nobody else knew we were there! 'Audley makes us feel cosseted,' says Hazel. 'They have taken us to the forts of Rajasthan, the temples of Jodphur and we have stayed in the most amazing of palaces.' No, that is not a typo – she said palaces and not places.

'Are you with Audley?' she repeats. I feel like saying, 'No, I'm with 'Pete's DIY Travel Services. Purveyors of the odd trip for people who shop at Aldi, buy clothes from Primark and like the odd fry-up with a pint of John Smith's bitter in departures.' It would seem the other British couple travels with Audley as well. Because when I say, 'No, we have planned the trip ourselves,' I'm sure the woman turned her shoulder away from us even more.

Michael and Hazel are pleasant lunch companions to chat with, totally amazed we would organise our trip ourselves, hardly believing it possible. Both this location and our previous homestay are all Audley Travel recommendations, apparently. I wonder if we are paying significantly less for the same experience as those with Audley, but without the support and backup? No meeting strangers at the airport with cash for them! Like us, after reading the itinerary, Michael and Hazel are taking the nature walk at 4:30 pm. We all start laughing and we agree to be late for the walk might not be a good idea.

The forests, river, and landscaped gardens of the homestay are stunning. Set on a hillside, the main house is impressive in its design and style. It's like I'm walking through some botanical gardens back in England. The land, sloping down from the house, hosts a small swimming pool and yoga area, to the meandering river where you can swim or punt a pontoon along.

At precisely 4:30 p.m., the group set off. The four French friends, Michael and Hazel, with Pete and Noreen bringing up the rear. There are a few cows, Vichuz tells us, to provide milk, and to convert their manure into methane for all the cooking. They feed the chickens pecking at my feet leftovers of our food. I feel relieved, as I could hardly eat a fraction of what they served for lunch, each mouthful exploding with taste. We saunter around the grounds, Vichuz pointing out this tree, that spice, and pulling peppercorns off a bush. 'Taste the difference between white, black, and red corns.' I pick up a white, then a black, and try to go for a red. 'Only two, only two,' he tells me.

We pass a bubbling pond. 'We farm fish here, but not the sort we feed tourists. You can't get any flavour into that kingfish we cook you; tourists always complain about the bones in our fish.' Heading to an area in an open-sided polytunnel, he points to piles of ginger and turmeric and with a sharp knife gives each of us a small piece. 'In America, they have found that turmeric can cure a multitude of illnesses. We knew that in India 5000 years ago.' He breaks into fits of giggles; it's something Vichuz does every time he cracks a joke. This makes me laugh, because it seems as if his jokes are funny to him. The way my dad jokes are to me.

Stupidly, and I can't remember what I said, I offer a witty retort. Like the scenes when tumbleweed blows across the desert, there is silence in the air. His white eyes dart my direction, and he holds a stare, looking at me longer than feels comfortable but saying nothing. Shrugging his shoulders, he carries on as if I had said nothing. Vichuz tells us to wait where we are and goes foraging under a bush and comes back with a fresh pineapple. I'm wondering if they hid it under a bush because he wouldn't let anyone go near him when he went to fetch it. I have to say it was probably the best pineapple I've ever tasted.

We all head back for a cookery demonstration taking place at 5:30 p.m. precisely. The kitchen is hotter than a vindaloo. The chef, flamboyant, loud, more Ainsley Harriott than Gordon Ramsay, is cooking up a storm. Adding this and that to the dishes, some clumsy person (me) leans on five stainless-steel rods that will spear chicken for the tandoori oven. They crash down on stainless-steel counters, stopping our chef midflow – everyone glares in my direction. The French ask hundreds of questions, all of which need translating. I'm hot, and I've heard enough. I thought at least we might have had a sample by now. Finally, the chef builds to a demonstration crescendo by signing a copy of his Indian cookbook. I get out of the kitchen, the heat too much for me.

The sound of London Dry Gin falling into a glass (a good measure) is a symphony of anticipation playing in the warm air as we sit on a balcony. They sell alcohol here. Where we are sitting, a cold wine and G&T in hand, opposite us is the strangest looking chair. There was one similar at the last home-stay, giggling as we remember Angela's comment when she saw it. Having a very short seat, the arms swing out allowing you to rest your feet and legs on them, reclining backwards. Angela said it reminded her of having a smear.

The teams of staff are laying tables below us in the courtyard for dinner; it looks beautiful. The food, as every meal during our stay, is sumptuous, served piping hot and always too much to eat. We find conversation awkward sitting next to people we don't know. Why is it the first question always seems to be, 'So, what do you do for a living?' My reply is often, 'I write about dead people.' It always provokes an interesting response. Vichuz crackles with laughter, saying, 'Don't the living not make better subjects?' before giggling at his own joke. I smile, hiding silent annoyance.

Turning to say hello to the new guest just arrived, now sitting next to me, she smiles back and says, 'Are you with Audley?'

Chapter 18

Vive la France

WANDERING THE GARDENS AT dawn feasts my eyes, ears, and nose. The air is heady with the musky damp perfume from uncountable flowers, the branches of endless trees are lined with exotic birds fighting to make their declaration rosebuds are here for the gathering today. Their anthem jubilant of life hangs heavy in the air around me it's so loud. Wandering down to the river in awe and gratefulness, I gather this moment, keeping it for another day. I try to be in this moment, fully present and soaking it all in. After writing for a little while, I walk the paths leading back towards the house; breakfast is at 8:30 a.m. Vichuz read me the rules when I arrived. What he didn't say was they would sound a gong as a reminder to obey. Echoing across the silence and tranquility I heard the call to breakfast.

We sit between Michael and Hazel and new guests David and Tina. Regular visitors to India, David and Tina are returning to Kerala for a second time. 'Are you with Audley?' The question is becoming all too common. 'When in India we only use Audley as a tour operator,' David says. 'Tina does all the research, then Audley book the accommodation and provide transport from place to place with a private driver and car staying with us for the trip.' I had considered hiring a driver and car for the whole of our trip. Chatting with both couples, it seems their drivers, 'our men,' are staying here as well. When we were on our nature walk, Vichuz pointed to dormitories where drivers stay and eat, ready and waiting for their clients to move on. Both couples spoke about how they knew their drivers, and their drivers learning what they liked and accommodating their needs. We book taxis to our next location. At around £10 for every hour driven, it makes transport relatively inexpensive, safe, and simple for us. So far.

Today we are joining the French group, along with David and Tina, heading out on a neighbourhood tour at 9:30 a.m. Michael was doing a longer nature walk – alone, his solitary sojourn this time because none of the other guests had chosen that route. It felt we had to choose some option. Vichuz was a bit surprised Hazel had decided she wanted to sit and journal. Giggling hysterically over some quip he cracked, he shrugged his shoulders and headed off towards the group of Australians.

9:30 a.m. – The neighbourhood tour should be starting.

9:30 a.m. and 30 seconds – Vichuz is missing a Frenchman.

9:31 a.m. – Eyes dart between Vichuz and his wife, who had arrived to wave everyone off. They look incredulous, though not surprised, four Brits and only three French are at the appointed place at the appointed time.

9:32 a.m. – Vichuz's demeanour is changing by the second.

9:33 a.m. – The tension is rising.

9:35 a.m. – One of the French wives shouts something up at the balcony. My French is basic, but it is something like:

'Faisons-les attendre Henri! Il leur a fallu trois ans ou plus pour régler le Brexit, nous allons les faire attendre un peu! Assurez-vous de mettre ce polo fuchsia! Vive La France!'

Translated – 'Let's keep them waiting, Henri! It took them three years or more to settle Brexit, we'll make them wait a bit for us! Make sure you put that fuchsia polo shirt on! Hurray for France!'

9:37 a.m. – Henri arrives, the collar of his Ralph Lauren (fuchsia) polo shirt nonchalantly turned up. His walking trousers look as if the delay was because he was pressing them, the seam as sharp as a knife. His baseball cap looks stylish in only the way maybe a Frenchman could make a baseball cap fashionable.

'Did I keep you all waiting?' Henri says in perfect English, without a trace of apology, embarrassment, or concern. 'Let's go,' he offers.

Vichuz issues some commands to the young guy leading the walk, and off we march. We haven't gone over 200 metres when Jean, Henri's meilleur ami, has to run back to the room; he'd forgotten something. A spray of Hermes aftershave, I guess. Meandering up the drive of the homestay, passing beehives, we see where they source the honey we eat for breakfast when Jean rejoins the group, out of breath but with the redolence of spices and citrus fruits wafting by.

There are rubber trees as far as we can see. Like spent, war-weary soldiers on parade identical distance between each trunk, they stand straight and scarred by the years of daily wounds lacerated into the wood flesh, chiselled a slice at a time, satisfying a thirsty world of its white sap.

Our guide is in his early 20s. He was born and lives in the village where we are heading. He tells me he is grateful for his job at the homestay, and he went to management school but wants to work in IT. He explains the 400 rubber trees a hectare need 'tapping' regularly to get the raw rubber. This natural liquid white gold is mixed with chemicals and makes blocks of latex for products we use day to day. Half coconut shells, slightly above head height, are collecting the precious sap on every tree.

Our group walks through a clearing between trees to a concrete shack, acrid smoke from a wood fire inside hanging in the air outside. The smell sticks in the back of my throat; it tastes of hardship. Around the back of this small house our guide is winding a rectangle block of latex through a series of rollers, thinning it each time. Like some pasta machine, the latex gets longer and thinner each time the mangle spits it out the other side. Herding us now into the run-down rectangle of concrete, Henri pushes his way to the front. Our guide shows the same teatowel-sized blocks are hanging up in the chimney being smoked to dry them in preparation for selling.

A frail woman, the severe twisted line of her mouth grimacing no hint of a smile, hides out of the way in a darkened room, her hand hanging to one side, weariness in its fall. She seems resigned to let this unknown, uninvited horde enter and wander around her home. A few sticks of broken furniture, a frayed thin bed mat on the floor, a mobile phone company calendar on the wall, odd days crossed out. Dented stainless steel pots stacked by the sink, dried red crumbs of rice sticking to the sides. But her home nonetheless. This is rural life in Kerala. I feel awkward being here, an unwelcome guest. Henri leads the group out. As we leave, I see our guide place a few rupees into her hand, still at her side. The daily intrusion of neighbourhood guests for her seems a source of welcome income as much as an unwanted interruption. It doesn't make me feel any better. Perhaps our intrusion into her life might make all the difference to her.

We walk a short distance to the rubber plantation where a homemade five-rung ladder lazily leans against a tree. 'Who wants to have a go a tapping a rubber tree?' our guide asks. I jump to the opportunity.

The tapper's weathered skin on his hands and face show signs of a lifetime of hard manual work. His smile shows joy and contentment in the toil. Tappers start at 4:00 a.m. each day, the sap running quicker when it's cool. They tap around 800 trees a day. Climbing the short rungs, a scalpel sharp chisel takes 2mm off the bark cut spiralling up the tree. Raw white rubber bleeds from the incision. Using tar and plastic, they protect this open wound on the tree to keep transfusing white gold. The tapper takes me to a 'practice tree', showing me the delicate angle and speed needed to slice the bark. I'm a natural, he tells me. He offers me a job. I decline. 'I enjoy writing about dead people, thank you,' I say.

We are taking a 'diversion' our guide says, because there are roadworks. The path through the forest takes us past more concrete huts where the tappers live, six families to a home. Tramping through bushes and over roots we exit onto a road directly opposite the team laying tarmac and into blinding sunlight. So much for the diversion. No ingenious roadlaying machines here. The still blanket of humid air cloaking us is heated higher. It's now oily, caustic, like coal tar soap plugging your nostrils. The road gang toil burning black tar on wide spades over open fires, tarmacking bucket by bucket. It's a scene from someone's version of hell. Relentless, four or five men rush back and forwards progressing the miles long road, one spade at a time. No wonder many roads here are potholed assault courses. I observe a glance between our guide and the labourers. I can't quite judge it. There is certainly an observation, but as if looking straight through, and beyond the humanity, no connection. It's as if they are not there.

We stroll single file along the road, crossing a bridge. It's clear when monsoon season arrives it becomes a flowing torrent, not the gentle stream we see looking over the railings. We enter a tiny village. It comprises of one street. Out of place, an impressive-looking school sits at the end of the street. Three floors high and many classes wide, it dominates the scene. The road falls away on each side to a few tangled shops.

Guided into the first, more a roughly built rectangle of space than a shop, a simple sewing machine sits silently alongside racks of brightly coloured fabric bundled on shelves. Against the far wall, making a modest changing room, they've pulled a curtain back where a red plastic chair sits and a mirror reflects us all squashed in anticipation, of what I'm not sure. Like the daily stop at the latex mangle, I'm guessing we are at another regular point of the 'tour.' Greeting us is a tailor who offers to run up a dress, sari or baggy pants suit overnight for the corralled tourists.

The two French women are in their element. Their spirits spark and voices crackle into life. Animated, loud, they pull fabric off the shelves, letting it fall, holding it against each other. The plain white trousers and simple t-shirt they wear are identical, like aged twins, and look chic somehow. They go about describing in French to the long-suffering woman in precise details the style and cut of the haute couture they want 'running up.' David and Tina sit patiently, swivelling the portable AC unit towards their direction. Wisely, they suspect this could be a long process. I would doubt even Coco Chanel took more time over her creations. Noreen browses, hoping to find something exciting or some unique fabric. Fed up, I wander out and along the street following Henri and Jean, who I guess have often waited together outside clothes shops.

Every other shop in the village is empty. Men hang around, as they seem to here in India, chatting and reading newspapers. I buy some Coke from a shop and head back to the emporium on the Champs Élysées.

Henri and Jean arrive as it's time to pay. Henri drives a hard bargain and knocks £1 off two dresses. I'm incensed. The time these two French women have taken, the work the tailor must do, and he knocks 50p off a dress! I trip him up as walks past me, smug as a snail cooked in garlic. Falling, his fuchsia pink Ralph Lauren polo shirt gets covered in brown dust and dirt. (OK, I didn't, but I sure felt like doing it.)

I get annoyed when I see this happen. I'm sure this local business is grateful for the constant supply of 'customers' brought directly to their door. There would be little other trade passing. I imagine money changes hands somewhere along the process. For sure the tailor who actually does the work will not get all the cash. To barter the life out of her, showing your delight, even smugness, that you have 'won' a better deal with such small sums of money seems unjust and unfair. It's inconsiderate tourism. There is forever the balance between being 'ripped off' as a tourist and considerate tourism. Already on this trip we sense the money we have been asked us for on occasion was 'tourist' rates. I've questioned prices, haggled a bit for tuk-tuk fares, then given the driver a tip more significant than what he was asking when he took care of us. You cannot equate value to the price – £3-£4 here is a day's pay for many. I guess it's having wisdom at the moment in not being taken advantage of, but just as much, not taking advantage of situations or people where making a living can be so hard.

At the opposite end of the one street is the bus stop – no sign, it's just where the bus stops. As part of our 'cultural experience,' we get to ride the local bus halfway back towards the homestay. The remaining stretch is by tuk-tuk. Perhaps for some guests, taken door to door by a private driver in a taxi, this will be a holiday experience remembered. For us, it was more interesting to observe how our fellow travellers responded.

The open-sided blue bus came speeding to a halt. Hordes of kids, dressed smart in pure white shirts and blue skirts and trousers, jostle past us, rushing to get the empty backseat. They hang out the glassless windows, smiling from the ringside view now gained. The two French women sidle to the front of the bus where only women can sit. Noreen and I stand holding a pole halfway down the bus.

We speed off in F1 start style. Flat-out, the driver navigates each bend. We began with one hand, but soon two doesn't seem enough. Wrapping our arms around the pole, Nemesis at Alton Towers Theme Park was a gentle ride compared to this adventure. Twisting, turning, left and right – not the bus, it's my stomach doing gymnastics. Battle-scarred after a few miles, we get off, Noreen relieved 'Pete's DIY Tours' hadn't decided on public transport rather than a taxi to get us from place to place. Later, that evening, it was interesting to hear some guests had been in India for three weeks, and it was the first time they had experienced a tuk-tuk. My first response is how unfortunate. What opportunities they had missed! Then I stop myself.

Who decides what's a rosebud and what isn't? Maybe a five-minute tuk-tuk is still a rosebud, because riding in an air-conditioned private taxi is 'de rigueur' when travelling abroad? Have they missed out? Or not? I don't think it's possible to judge another's contentment in life. If writing hundreds of eulogies has taught me anything, it's there is no such thing as normal, no measure of life to which you can align which one can say is best for all. By the roll of the dice of life, the place and position of our birth could be different. By genes and opportunity, choices we have freely taken may have been available or refused to another. One man's misery could be another's contentment. Some lives who seem by material measures wealthy are bereft of connection – others with little above meal to meal survival are rich beyond measure. So, a rosebud is a rosebud, when we experience it. The critical action is to gather it when we do.

Back at the homestay a frantic screeching broke the solitude of our afternoon swimming, reading, and resting. The tormenting sound of an animal in pain, by our guess. On and on it went, chilling to the ears. A tuk-tuk went past with a large goat in the backseat tied in, but still shrieking. Thinking it was off to market, it worried us. (Concerned as the goat was, I bet.) Thankfully, he returned in the same tuk-tuk, much quieter, about an hour later. I think they'd took it for a ride for the 'cultural experience.'

We rest until gin o'clock. Tonight someone else bagged the doctor's examination chair, so we sit downstairs as hundreds of candles were lit star shape in the courtyard to light the dining tables.

Next to Noreen sat Vichuz's wife. She tells us a little of life for them. For 35 years, Vichuz had been a respected engineer until he retired to come and look after the family land. Vichuz was the eighth son. It was his responsibility to take on this responsibility; his wife's responsibility was to take on her elderly parents-in-law. While quirky, direct, and abrupt, just as much Vichuz was welcoming, kind, and open. Vichuz runs a tight operation – there is a pervading excellence in everything around us. The engineer's attention to detail, maybe, has built a remarkable business. The routines, fixed agendas, Vichuz keeps things tightly controlled, ensuring the repeatable quality of experience for all tourists, I suppose. It works. Though everything is too 'packaged' for us, it is hard to criticise.

Dressed in matching staff saris, four women are sweeping the leaves from the courtyard as we sit down to eat. Our dinner is magnificent; the chickens will eat well tomorrow.

The evening conversation flows easier. I see a book on the table David is reading and ask him about it. He tells me it's a tome about Churchill, and we chat animatedly together about Winston. I'm fascinated to listen to the stories people tell about their lives. Not sure why, at this particular moment, but I ask him what would be on the soundtrack of his life. This question sets off a fascinating glimpse into his past. He talks of his love for jazz and rock, but suddenly stops midsentence. Then, poignantly, tells me a story about the Frank Sinatra song High Hopes. Dabbing his eyes with a napkin, the mere mention of 'high apple pie hopes,' opened the door to his granaries of the past. Both deep joy and unresolved pain were between the sentences of his story. It only takes the opening notes of a song to do the same for each of us.

I thought rosebuds could only be found in places, people and possessions. Reflecting on David's story, I see rosebuds can be found in songs and music as well. The soundtrack to my life, now I think about it, is like the record shops of old. The ones where you flicked the LPs forward, a singer or a group at a time, but now a story at a time. I can stand in the granaries of my past, hear a song and instantly be taken back to a time, a place or a person.

'The Sun Has Got His Hat On' by Ambrose and His Orchestra, reminds me of my earliest memories of dad singing and dancing around the house. The soundtrack of my childhood was played on a Dansette record player – 'Needles and Pins,' by The Searchers, 'Spanish Flea,' by Herb Alpert and his Tijuana Brass. 'Downtown,' by Petula Clark, and 'In The Summertime' by Mungo Jerry. The first songs I bought were two 45 rpm singles. There was, 'Fanfare For The Common Man,' by Emerson, Lake and Palmer, along with, 'Can't Live' by Harry Nielsen. The couple who lived next door would play Elvis Presley records. I would go around and listen to Elvis sing, 'Teddy Bear' along with Simon and Garfunkel singing 'Bridge over Troubled Water.'

Then a miracle came along – the Walkman. It was unbelievable you could carry music around with you, being wired for sound. Abba, Mike Oldfield, Jean-Michel Jarre and T-Rex were among the accompaniment to my teenage angst. So was Jean Genie, Space Oddity, Sorrow, and Life on Mars by David Bowie. I'm sure it's listening full blast to Status Quo on my wired headphones is why I now need hearing aids.

That evening, in the glow of hundreds of candles, six strangers found common ground in many places. And not discussing what we do for work, or whether or not we are with Audley.

Noreen and I have wondered if we are we group travel people. We have considered future travels to off the beaten track places joining a small group trip. On reflection, we're not. Listening between the lines of the adventures in palaces and forts, there was a recognition from the conversation days were too busy, many times not getting enough freedom to wander, seeking those spontaneous memory-making 'rosebud' moments travel can serendipitously bring. Getting lost down a back alley, drinking tea with the locals, getting to know, albeit slightly, more of the place you are visiting – not 'on the coach', – 'off the coach', – 'on the coach' days. But there again, for others it may be an adventure full of rosebuds. That's the thing about them, you have to gather your own.

Tomorrow we head for the hills, to tea country and Munnar Town.

Heading away from the table, Vichuz shouts to me climbing shoeless silent to our room, 'Mr Peter, don't forget your taxi will be here at 9:30 am sharp.'

CHAPTER 19

SMOKE GETS IN YOUR EYES

IT'S PRECISELY 9:30 A.M. Waving goodbye to Vichuz and his wife bumping, jolting, and lurching in complete luxury. We can't believe we are in an Audley Travel taxi.

The day began with reveille, as hundreds of birds were bugling their wake-up call. Noreen slumbers on. Hot brown dust coffee in the mug. Writing set up. I enjoy the quiet cold of this part of the day.

The gong sounds for breakfast. We scurry downstairs, ready to clock in. Leaving the requisite share for the chickens to feed on, we say our goodbyes to new guests staying. We can hear them deciding which of the items on the laminated itinerary they will do. I think Vichuz wants them out of the way for a while either way.

Settling our bill, Vichuz quips something about writing for the living and the dead, falling about laughing at his superb wit and candour. I say, (and I really do) 'I will write about you while you are alive, Vichuz. I promise I will.' Passing over the cash, I see he's adding the cost of the taxi to Munnar. The rate is like what we have been paying, £10 for every hour of travel. Munnar is about 70 miles East and uphill, so 3,500 INR seems about right. Nothing there betrays the surprise coming our way. The ever-helpful staff bring our bags down from the room, loading them into a white Toyota Innova.

Noreen poses for a leaving photo with Vichuz's wife. Dressed in a striking fuchsia pink sari, with a black contrasting scarf, she is heading to work. As sharp as Vichuz, she wants to know where we had been, what the occupancy was like, where we are going next. Had we heard if this virus thing was stopping people travelling. She was gentle in her interrogation, absent of abruptness. She was genuine, with an open interest in us, the conversation punctuated with one of those beautiful Indian smiles.

I see Vichuz is getting itchy – 9:30 a.m. is arriving fast. A hand hovering over the gleaming chrome door handle belongs to a tall, handsome driver, his shirt brilliant white. He waits patiently. Vichuz motions to the car, encouraging us in. The door opens and we enter another world.

Sounds dramatic, for sure, but the interior is chilled to perfection, like a good Kingfisher beer. The car's temperature is as ice-cold as the bottles of water in door bins, beads of condensation running down the outsides. We get comfy on pristine white cotton seat covers, piped in blue. Between us, is a 'goodie' box. It's filled with biscuits, nuts, juice, and, delighting Noreen, cans of cold Coke. I am surprised to find hanging from the back of the driver's seat in front of me is a personal letter from the founder of Audley Travel. Is there some kind of mistake? Do they think we are with Audley?

'Dear Guest,' the letter begins. 'Experience a journey of Perfect Moments, (the perfect moments capitalised for emphasis) instants that endure and leave a lasting positive impression...' In closing, 'We wish you a very comfortable journey with us, Craig Burkinshaw, Founder of Audley Travel.'

Thanks, Craig, we will!

We snap selfies. My face is looking smug. But not as smug as a certain Frenchman – our négociateur extraordinaire.

Our driver could take the lead in a Bollywood movie. I'm guessing, but I think he is the driver of a guest at staying at the homestay. I imagine them on parade by now, marshalled into ranks, ready for the neighbourhood walk. He speaks excellent English and tells us he works for a travel company in Cochin. Married, with two young children, it's been five weeks since he has seen his home. Life is hard. Hard here for most, it seems. Because however much this taxi costs, they will share the money out between a few, leaving minimum wage for the driver. We climb towards the plantations, watching mountains and mist appear and the view disappear. So, I turn a page on the book I'm trying to read before we get to Munnar.

A tea plant, left to mature, grows to a height of twenty feet. Its beautiful white blossoms resemble those of the camellia, along with a refreshing fragrance. For commercial cultivation, they keep tea bushes low by periodical pruning, and maintained at the height of four feet to form an optimum 'plucking table.' I gain these pearls of information from a fascinating book called 'An Elephant Kissed My Window (And other stories from tea plantations in South India)' by M Ravindran and Saab Aggarwal.

The history of British involvement in India is intrinsic to the history of our favourite brew. In 1833, an expatriate Brit noted camellia bushes grew prolific high in the hills. Ordering a few tea seeds from China, the growing of tea in India began. The mountains of South India are lush with plantations. The spices of various kinds, rubber, and coffee, we had seen grow at lower altitudes. But tea thrives higher up. The best bouquet comes from tea estates at 3500 to 8000 feet. We climb steep passes for the best part of our journey over the next four hours.

The driver navigates hairpin bends on our route with ease. The road twisting and turning back on itself, interspersed with severe straight steep climbs. He needs to use first gear most of the way. Forever winding upwards, the road is crossing ravines and bridges; the atmosphere changing, mist obscures the ranges of hills shrouded in the distance. On and on we climb.

The scenery changes, yet the sights of rural India stay the same. Roadside kiosks, battered buildings, wares spilling for sale out over the dust. Hoardings advertising mobile 4G networks. Billboards displaying enticing wedding jewellery families will rent but most only dream of buying.

Manicured terraces of tea are cut like a giant's steps down the mountain. Deep green, the pickers' lines visible on hillsides full of bushes resemble contour lines drawn on a map showing the severity of the slopes. Tea bushes hug the entire landscape. The hill town and plantation area of Munnar comes into view. Turning off the main road, a pot holed track takes us through lines of tea, passing pickers bagging the day's clippings, until we arrive at the hotel where we stay for the next couple of days.

Influencing the way I planned 'Pete's DIY' trip to India was James Wallman's book, 'Time and How to Spend It.' I found the book a riveting, if not easy, read. It was one of those books which takes reading and rereading again for deeper understanding. The précis of the book argues we plan much of our work time, but often leave our leisure time to chance. Or worse, never consider it. Too tired from working, we end up crashing out in front of the T.V. or mindlessly waste time online. Wallman proposes planning our time around the mnemonic device S.T.O.R.I.E.S. by focusing on experiences over possessions, building stronger relationships, and creating vivid memories to find increased happiness in our days. As the writer Annie Dillard says, 'How we spend our days is, of course, how we spend our lives.' I want to remember as many as mine as I can, and who doesn't want to bring happiness into their lives? It sounds a lot like the idea of gathering rosebuds to me.

In a chapter on planning holidays, Wallman introduces a few ideas on how to build memorable times into your trips. For example, some people he suggests choose a holiday to 'fly and flop.' These are holidays only sitting on a beach or by a pool to relax. In truth, sometimes it feels just what you need. While these types of holidays are enjoyable, he argues, they struggle to create lasting memories. Are rosebuds scarce to find around a pool for a week or so? I'm not sure; a week by a pool is something I've enjoyed in the past. Especially when the family was young – hours of 'Watch me dad!' are splashed full of rosebuds.

For me now, however, curious about people and places, and wanting to fill the granaries up, travelling miles to a sit around a pool or be on a beach feels like I'm missing out. I want to explore, enriched by surprises, in awe of unfamiliar sounds, smells, and places. I want to experience things new and unexpected. I want to go gathering unexpected rosebuds while I can. Because out of these kind of experiences come stories.

We all end up as a story someone tells. Travel experiences, for me, are one way to write a different story about my life. We remember 'scenes' from our life rather than actual moments.

We see our lives by capturing snapshots of events in the past. 'Flying and flopping' alone, for me now, does not make memorable holidays, because you don't have too many stories to tell about the time passed. As the years of our life progress, we don't have fresh stories or rosebuds to add to the storehouse of our lives. Wallman suggests it can be much more memorable than that. It's the irregular, unexpected, and different we remember looking back over life. The truth is most of life is forgettable. But when we plan and design better experiences for our holidays, our memories of these times can bring lasting happiness in many unique ways.

Planning 'Pete's DIY Tours' India trip was built around times and places where we would explore, unsure what we would find, making the days unpredictable. Moving on, other days would be to rest, relaxing in different accommodation, days reading, swimming, and taking it easy. After all, that's what part of a holiday is about, whatever Wallman writes! Trying to get the mix balanced, however, will be other days where experiences are a priority.

After the first week of busy activities, we planned to have a few days in stunning and beautiful locations and stay in distinctive hotels. If serendipity plays its hand while we are there, fantastic. If we just spend days reading and swimming, that's OK too. The hotel in Munnar was one such unique place on our itinerary.

Perching a hotel on the hillside overlooking waterfalls must have been a logistical, architectural, and expensive challenge! The result is stunning. A few miles out of Munnar, this hotel was a treat for the eyes.

As we arrive, porters dressed as smart as soldiers on parade lift our bags out of the car. Two young women adorned in beautiful white and gold saris anoint our heads with sandalwood paste and hand over two red roses while namaste greeting us to the hotel.

It has been one of the most noticeable aspects of India, and the places we have visited so far – people want to please and take care of us. Even Vichuz in his unique way. He was quirky and abrupt sometimes, but never rude, yet making sure we had the best experience in India while staying there mattered to him. You could see attention to detail everywhere. Yes, of course, we are in a hotel, so you could say it is their job. I've stayed in many hotels where it felt as if you were hindering someone from working rather than being their guest who they want to please. At this hotel, for example, we were staying on the first floor. Rather than waiting for a lift each time, we walked the few steps down to the pool or restaurant. Each time, reaching the reception level, all the staff would stand, bring their hands together – 'Namaste' – greeting us. They must have been up and down all day.

Our room is on the first floor. There were six below as well. It is spacious and beautifully appointed, with an enormous bed and a dining table. The view from the small balcony, toilet, and shower is stunning, looking over the river and out across tea plantations as far as you could see. We unpack. We can trash a hotel room in minutes. We take a photo quickly when we arrive because soon cases, books, and the contents of backpacks will fill the space.

We wander around the hotel. From a viewing platform lounge the rush of water gushing downwards fills waterfalls below. An infinity swimming pool hung out over the edge of the cliff gives unprecedented views of the location — a stunning place to stay. We recognise how blessed we are, so stop and breathe in the moment, truly grateful for the opportunity. We swim, drink coffee, read, and have a nap before an afternoon trip to Munnar.

Waiting in reception for our tuk-tuk to arrive, reception staff take their seats yet again, the concierge hovering by the door looking up the track away from the hotel. Open-sided, driven with motorbike handles, they are noisy, smelly, uncomfortable, and incredible fun. They negotiate bumps, potholes, and rough roads better than a four-wheel jeep, but on three wheels. Our chariot arrives, but stays beyond the boundary of the hotel car park. He has no choice.

We are heading to Munnar town, some fifteen minutes' jolt down the road. We find it – it's filthy, a ramshackle, sprawling, noisy, and forgettable place. We wandered around a bit, the object of stares and few smiles. The shrine where the driver dropped us was a collection of Christian and Hindu symbols, the aroma of incense hanging in the air mixed with the stench of diesel fumes. Like silent swarms of bees, black and yellow tuk-tuks queue at every spare space of road. How they get enough work is a mystery. Is this why most of the drivers are asleep in the backseats? No trade today, and little possibility?

It blights the beauty of the surrounding mountains and hills by the way the town has expanded over the years. Corrugated steel shacks spread out from a manic centre street, not much more there than a cacophony of horns blaring. It must be cultural acceptance here to throw rubbish wherever. Munnar feels like visiting a rubbish dump with a few random stalls. It's not lost on me a huge number of people call it home. Neither is the thought far away, should I be able to chat with locals, there would be rosebuds for gathering among the discarded remnants of life littering everywhere I look. Even here one man's mess is another's garden to harvest. You could fall in the rubbish and come up smelling of rosebuds. It's a matter of perspective, choice, and attitude.

We can live blinded. Behind every struggle there is the scarcity of hope. Every struggle. Frankl implores me to remember everything can be taken away from me: my food, my clothes, my home, my family, even my very breath and yet, 'the last of the human freedoms' is to decide the choice of what I see left, and my choice of attitude in the moment. The ultimate rosebud for gathering is my willingness, even in the face of tragedy, to search for the space between overwhelming grief and loss and choose my response. In response lies my freedom or servitude.

Heading down back alleys, side streets, and through odd basement bazaars, the town reveals its dark underbelly of despair.

Sad faces peddle a few overripe fruits. Costing few rupees, pakora and bhajis covered in flies and heated by the sun spearing the darkness offering for free the potential of swift visits to the bathroom later. Old men, crippled legs struggling to keep them standing, their knees knots of pain and inflammation standing out like lumps in tattered ropes, offer us garlands to buy for temple worship. Bags of spices spill out onto dirt. People fill the gap between stalls and traffic. No pavements here. We pass a local 'comfort station.' I'm glad we went before we left the hotel and had not eaten the pakora. We stand to watch a jeweller working on the street, shaping and working a gold ring, holding it in his toes like a vice. Nobody hassles us to buy anything. There is nothing we would want to buy anyway. Passing the only other white couple we see, silently we acknowledge each other. We've seen enough. We decide to head back; the hotel is too lovely not to make the most of our stay. We found a tuk-tuk. Or I should say he found us.

I once read a rule of travel safety: don't be a customer of someone who is looking for customers. He was on the lookout for any business. His smart and crisp clean white shirt stood out among the grey of the streets, he had a friendly face, so I nodded acceptance and we hopped in. We tell him where we want to go. He pivots in the middle of the road, avoiding being hit by some miracle, and we buzz towards the hotel.

The driver was indeed a good guy. I think most people in the world are. There are of course as many mad axe-murderers overseas as there are at home. But I've found more rosebuds meeting with local people than staying with tourists. We chat for a while – eyes meeting in the rear-view mirror, turning to speak over his shoulder. The virus has scared everyone away, he tells us, worry etched on his face. And then stopped speaking, lost in his thoughts.

We grind the couple of miles out of Munnar, turning onto the hotel road, where he stops. I watch him invite an old lady to sit next to him in the front. She was visibly struggling to carry three heavy plastic sacks with handles, too large to be called bags. Reluctantly, she hands him her burdens, shoehorning herself next to them with little space for her to sit, not glancing once to the backseat. Considering the heat of the day, she was cold-faced. Though we couldn't understand his conversation, he had a cheeky way with him which needed no translation.

He beamed a smile her direction. I hear 'auntie,' and soon she was laughing and giggling along with his words, the four of us swaying in unison, missing potholes. We all arrive shaken well at the hotel. He stops the tuk-tuk just outside the tarmac of the hotel car park. We tip him well.

Standing to greet us at the door of the hotel, the hotel concierge welcomes us back, his hands together in a prayer. In the background a receptionist stands, hands clasped in supplication our way. 'We have entertainment tonight in the hotel on the third floor; it is fire dancing, will you come?' he says.

'Sounds too good to miss,' I say, serendipity sensors going into overdrive.

The third floor was not open-air, more suited to a conference meeting than promised fire dancing. The hotel's occupancy was emptying quick, though we were unaware how many guests were leaving and heading to airports and to overseas homes at the time. It surprised us when an intimate group of nine people gathered for the spectacle.

We sidled into the second row. Lights dim, music blares, volume at maximum, as it seems set for everything here. Swaying out of the dark, we see the shape of a man who had eaten far too many poppadoms over his life. His back is to us, gyrating to dance music thumping in my ears. I switch my hearings aids off. He's moving back and forth like a seasoned boy band lead singer. 'Smokey,' as I shall call him, moved as seductively as a hammer peeling a banana.

Smokey removed a black leatherette waistcoat, dangling it from side to side. Then, throwing it off, he jumps, well hops, 180 degrees to face us. Next, his shirt flies far away in a frenzy of ripples exposing his physique, – well-rounded – and evidencing a diet of basmati rice and naan bread may not be the best for building muscles. The seams on his skintight red plastic trousers strain to keep everything in and together. The Tom Jones song 'You Can Leave Your Hat On' plays in my mind as a straw trilby stays fixed atop of his head below a face painted with white tribal looking swirls. Swaying this way and that, he thrusts his ample hips to a clip of 'Bad' by Michael Jackson. 'Who's Bad?' If not bad, he's certainly misbehaved – 'Smokey' is giving 110% as they would say on Britain's Got Talent, limited though his 'all' was. Did it get better, well... no – but different.

From the corner of the room, Smokey pulls out four sticks, four flames burning bright on the ends. He licks one end while trailing a spiral of thick fog smoke the other. The acrid smell of paraffin or lamp oil infuses the room. Long flames are shooting this way and that; I can't imagine another time when indoor fire dancing displayed so much enthusiasm. Simon Cowell would have loved it. Like the mists over the Munnar hills as we arrived earlier in the day, the high ceiling of the room could not stop the now descending clouds of white fumes. Nothing was deterring Smokey. On and on, his hips not lying, thrusting and twirling. Sucking on the flames, Smokey must have no worries about heartburn.

The music stopped. Smokey disappeared 'offstage.' I turn and say to Noreen, 'Let's go. I can't breathe!' Thinking she will jump at the chance, I am shocked to see she is looking transfixed. It must have been shock. Laughing, I say, 'You want to stay?' There was no time to answer. Smokey returned up close and personal with the audience, spitting fire now. Flame throwing fuel flew from his mouth, blasts of fire stretching across the small space. Not happy with the amount of applause, he stands, beckoning more. I'm worried any minute Noreen is going to rise out of her seat and shout, 'Bravo, bravo!'

The climax takes our breath away. It's that or the smoke, I'm not sure which. 'Take That' and, with a flurry of fire, he extinguishes all the flames with his mouth. It's disconcerting why smoke alarms are not sounding around the hotel. We head off to bed. I tell Noreen she has the aroma of a well-smoked kipper about her. She tells me I smell like a garden bonfire. Maybe as well as rosebuds in places, people, possessions and sounds, I could add smells to the list?

We make decisions about experiences anticipating an odd rosebud we might gather. Travel affords the unexpected. While I will remember the hotel room overlooking tea terraces, bowing, supplicating staff wanting to satisfy every need, and sumptuous food. These were in some ways expected by the choice of hotel we made, but I'll never forget Smokey.

While some rosebud gathering can be planned it's the spontaneous, unexpected kind appearing from curiosity and adventure enrapturing us the most. Will tomorrow's planned excursion back in time deliver more?

Chapter 20

Why Not Join Us at The Club?

There is an aroma filling the bedroom. Not the glorious redolence of fresh coffee, no, more the pungent stench of paraffin oil smoke. Our clothes reek. I stir, wondering how 'Smokey' gets his waistcoat and leather look trousers free of the smell. Not a good thought to hold first thing.

Breakfast is a grand occasion. The view across the valley from our table is breathtaking. Waiters and waitresses dressed in floppy hats, like a chef's but squashed over on one side, run around caring for our every wish. They introduce dosas, a rice flour crepe. The range of vegetable curries, rice, and spicy soups available seems a strange mix next to my boring toast and marmalade. In the restaurant's corner, a chef cooks eggs to order. Ever one for adventure, I go for that classic Indian meal – scrambled eggs on toast! Noreen opts for the dosa and scoffs it with enthusiasm. We plan a morning slowly sliding away, swimming, reading, and drinking coffee. This afternoon, we're off to explore a British institution, The Gymkhana Club, or Planter's Club.

Job adverts in London's high society gazettes painted the life of a tea plantation manager in India as exciting to those seeking employment in the further reaches of the Empire, a life full of adventure just waiting for the right young man. Along with the company house, staff would take care of everything you need. There is wildlife in abundance: elephants, panthers, buffaloes, and antelopes to come and shoot for sport. At the turn of the 20th century, young and privileged men would travel the seas to India. Plantation managers would take up posts high in the Munnar Hills working for British and Scottish tea companies such as Harrison Estates. What these enticing adverts failed to mention was how isolated living on a plantation could be. The odd motorbike accessed roads not passable by car, but mostly by foot, bullock cart, or horseback. For many of these expat British, the 'local' Gymkhana Club or Planter's Club (which could be many miles away) would be forever a bit of England in Indian for them.

I came across an article about an old Gymkhana Club or Plantation Club still open in Munnar. Contacting the club, they advised me rooms were available to stay (though I didn't need one) and they served food at certain times. What caught my eye most were the rules and regulations attached to the reply, including strict dress code for evenings. Intriguing. I couldn't wait to visit this bit of history in the area.

Turning a sharp right off the smooth main road, our tuk-tuk driver bumped and jostled us along a single-track road hugging the hillside parallel to the river that runs through Munnar. In the early 1900s, flooding even this high in the hills washed away most of what was a small tea processing town then. The driver seemed surprised when I asked him to take us to the club. He drove off quickly, not looking back after dropping us outside.

The club was a single-storey white building with a weathered red roof, looking across manicured flowerbeds. A gardener on hands and knees nods to us. Framing the grand entrance porch, bright purple bougainvillea spills down a waterfall of colour, its branches spilling across the floor. Standing to attention were a battalion of bright orange marigolds in terracotta pots positioned on steps, as well as on benches and platforms around the building. Comparing to the piles of rubbish, dilapidated shacks, and fumes of Munnar we can see, beyond a small golf course, this club is an oasis of calm, a watering hole of beauty in a desert of dirt. Posing for a couple of photos outside, tourists after all, we take one step forward inside and go back 100 years in time.

This Gymkhana Club, or Planter's Club, was started in 1905, 'For the gentlemen planters of the High Range in Kerala,' so the website history of the club recounts. In the year 1910 the High Range Club was formally completed. The clubhouse was immaculate and still carefully maintained. Sturdy wooden entrance doors pushed open with effort into a large high ceiling room.

Placed neatly around the edge of the highly polished floor, on rectangles of moss green carpet, were groups of polite conversation centres. Round rattan tables, two-seater couches, and low teak chairs, their arms polished by dinner jacket sleeves, filled the spaces, their dented and puffed-up feather cushions betraying many years of offered support. Painted in neat white script, each table, sofa, and chair had a number – HRC LL 63 and so on. The room echoed with silence. We were not alone. Sitting to the left were four Indian gentlemen, expensive suits, starched white shirts without ties. Sipping tea from white monogrammed cups, they look bewildered when we walked in. I say hello, they say nothing. A single finger points the way towards a doorway opposite. Shoes squeaking across the expanse of the room breaks the moment, and we head in the direction of the finger.

Lining the walls of interior corridors clustered black and white photos painting thousand-word portraits. A smiling young man is kneeling next to his trophy, a 'man-eating' tiger. Head lifted, its angry eyes stare at the treasured rifle still in his hand. I studied the faces in the next photo, entitled, 'A Sunday meet, Kundaly Club, 1930s.' The small group are dressed in military style jackets with white jodhpurs and are resting on a hillside. At the rear, a lone woman, pith hat tilting upwards, unable to contain her curls, smiles for the camera. The picture of a morning gathering, about 20 miles from here in the hills, seems to fulfil all the promises of those glossy magazine adverts.

Further along the corridor, on a large black wallboard, is the roll call of the Chairman and Honorary Secretary of the club. Sign painting the names in gold, the list begins in 1909. Revealing India's colonial history, the surnames start changing in the 1960s and 70s.

The air is cool, and with no natural light in the corridor, it's a welcome break from the heat outside. The same I imagine for many who would have gathered here. I see an opening ahead with the word, 'Steward' above. Looking through a wooden hatch, the countertop gleaming polished by thousands of hands, I see a lone man sitting at a desk. 'Can we order some lunch please?' I ask. Shaking his head, I needed to have booked the day before, he then kindly offers, 'But I can get them to make you a sandwich.' We wander back to the lounge passing the bar door where faded white paint commands, 'Men Only.' I want to see what is behind there.

We sit a couple of tables away from the local group, still bewildered by their looks and conversations our way. After a few minutes, a waiter, dignified in his gait, his shoes now breaking the uncomfortable silence, begins squeaking across the floor. Dressed in a white uniform, brass buttons, and a white pillbox hat, he walks as a soldier on parade. On one arm rests our lunch on a tray of monogrammed white china cups, side plates, and silver spoons. Placing them with great care, almost in slow motion on the low table where we are sitting, he asks if there was anything else we needed. There isn't. Bowing, he leaves, in the same manner I imagine he has done thousands and thousands of times before. The coffee is the best I have had in India – no brown dust here. The cheese and tomato sandwiches, crusts cut off – you would expect nothing less – are fresh and tasty. In previous centuries they transported England to India, and it is still here. Eating lunch, and reading for a while, I can't settle. My curiosity is unabated. I need to head off and explore what is behind that door.

I head to the toilets more for the opportunity to explore than anything else. Impossible to do unnoticed, the squeaks betraying my movement. The gentleman's cloakroom looks and feels unaltered little from the day it was built 100 years or more ago. Wooden lockers stained on the sides of doors by the sweat of hands playing tennis or golf, left traces of times past. Polite notices from the steward advise behaviour expected at all times in the club. Painted in gold copperplate lettering, a perceptive sign describes the personality of a man by the way he urinates. A nod at the humour of 'gentlemen planters' I'm guessing.

I walk back down the corridor, but the door to the bar is closed, and seems locked. Peering through the glass window, my curiosity wants to investigate further. Though tightly shut on the clasp, I notice the padlock is open. I'm staring at this when a waiter suddenly comes from behind opening the bar door. I sidestep him. 'Can I go in?' I ask. 'No,' he says. Thinking it was the camera hanging around my neck, I head to Noreen and leave it on the table. Then squeak back.

Exploring around the silent empty corridors some more, I see a billiards room – locked too. They've covered the green baize with a large dust cloth. On the walls are antelope and bullock heads, their lifeless icy stares waiting for the next game to begin. As I turn to leave, I see the white-suited waiter who had served us opening the bar door wide and I follow him in. I try again, 'Is it OK to look around?' He doesn't answer me, so this time I walk in, silence giving consent.

Wood panel walls lined with more animal heads have soaked in the conversations of a 100 years. An enormous bison's head sits in the centre. I wonder how many years he has been watching over the members drinking pink gins. Highly polished sporting trophies for cricket, polo, golf, fencing, and tennis are in glass cases, and on many shelves around the walls. A museum of victories. A wall contains a gallery of signed photos from navy ships. On the opposite wall is a collection of pith helmets. Arranged in a rainbow shape, the names of the previous owners are written in black on the edge of each hat. W. O. Milne was the first planter to hang his hat after 30 years continuous membership of the club – it seems the tradition continues today. The same names in white on a noticeboard underneath.

A single photo captures my attention. The scene is the bar many years before. Smart-suited men, ties this time, with dark tortoiseshell glasses, have drinks and cigars in hand. They stand where I am standing. In the background, three women sit demurely, legs crossed in politeness and observing the scene. What was this special occasion when they allowed women in the bar, I wonder? If the bison could speak, he would tell so many fascinating stories about this room. I wish I could hear them. Who are these men? What about those women? What was the social life of an expat like in the Plantation Club then? Fascinating. Curiosity abated, for a time, I squeak back.

The white-suited waiter returns with our bill. Handing me a receipt book, carbon copies in triplicate, he asks me to sign it. The cost? It was about £2, of which 50p was my subscription as a non-member. For this price, it was a captivating afternoon.

We decide to walk the short distance along a rough track back to Munnar Town. The unmade road passes carbon copy houses built the same time as the club and a derelict school. Three tea pickers, long tough leather aprons, baskets ready, are walking towards us, heading for the rows of tea growing above. From a distance, we can see a football match taking place in the town. A small crowd is watching pitchside inside the ground, whereas hundreds are standing on the roofs of tuk-tuks, buildings, buses, and houses trying to catch a glimpse who is winning outside for free. We decide we have seen enough of Munnar. Grabbing cold drinks from a shack of a store, we stand by the road.

We look like we are waiting for a ride. Never a good idea. Suddenly, a filthy, dilapidated tuk-tuk spins in the middle of the road to the annoyance of the horn blaring traffic it causes to swerve. Up front an unshaven bulk of a man, with no observable neck, asks where we are going. Sitting in the back, a small pretty girl is smiling at us. We barter a price back to the hotel. He tries hard to overcharge us. Relenting to a more reasonable price, the little girl then moves to the front, joining her dad, we learn, as he jolts us all towards the hotel.

At every stretch of the journey, he attempts selling us tours – a trip to the waterfalls. No thanks. A health massage – you must be kidding. Trying anything to make a sale. Trade here disappeared within weeks. No worries about offending us; we are captive passengers anyway. The season is ending, he tells us, but the fear of the virus is scaring any remaining tourists away. He makes no sale today apart from the fare, and a generous tip.

It is no surprise standing to greet us at the door of the hotel, the concierge is welcoming us back. 'Namaste,' he says, his hands still together in a prayer style. 'We have entertainment tonight in the hotel on the third floor. It is cultural dancing, will you come?' 'Sounds too good to miss,' I say, my serendipity sensors now going into turbodrive.

A delicious evening meal lazed over causes us to arrive late to the entertainment we hear taking place three floors above. The crowd is smaller than last night, and not wanting to interrupt the performance, we stand in the doorway, captivated.

Kathakali is a classical Indian dance form of Hindu performance art in Kerala. Its ancient traditions of conveying emotions, and telling its stories, are through intricate footwork, and particularly through facial gestures and eye movement. Kathakali takes human emotions difficult to put into words and puts them into dance. A way of reflecting rosebuds in movement, perhaps?

Distinguishing male actor-dancers, their elaborate colourful makeup and face masks takes hours to apply. Black cheeks, bright lime-green faces, coral-red lips, each colour representing good or evil, gods or demons, hunters or forest inhabitants.

Our dancer tonight is a young woman, a gold, blue, yellow and saffron whirl of energy as she moved across the floor. She dances full of passion and skill, stamping her feet, the bells on her ankles and bangles on her wrists beating a continuous rhythm in time with stirring music filling the space where smoke clouded us the night before.

Holding a bronze trident aloft, darting it one way, then another, she attacks and retreats in battle poses. Throwing her weapon behind, it's now her fists clenched tight, standing sure, a fearless warrior. I notice her platted black hair, interwoven with white and bright orange garlands, is hanging down as far as her knees. For a moment she stands still, gazing at her fingers now moving as if they were independent, having a mind of their own. Pointing, bending, pairing, splitting off alone, and all the time, head perfectly still, her bright eyes wide open, capturing this curious mystery before her.

Then it was over.

Over too soon. A bit like life.

Chapter 21

You Can Look but No Touch

CHICKEN, VEGETABLE, OR FISH curry for breakfast? I'm thinking – 75 miles of uneven roads ahead – a cheese omelette, while not a 'daring adventure,' could be the wise choice.

Leaving the dining room, the maître d'hôtel asks if we would be willing to fill in a survey on the service we received at the hotel. Five 'excellent' boxes ticked. A waitress takes it from us and places it into an envelope and seals it.

At reception, our bags carried down for us, again the head receptionist asks if we would be willing to fill in a survey on the service we received at the hotel. Six 'excellent' boxes this time ticked (again), she places it into an envelope before sealing it.

While waiting for the taxi (in reception about four steps from where we were at the desk a moment ago) the concierge politely asks us to fill in a survey on the service we received. The 'excellent' boxes ticked (this time back to four but on an iPad), we decide this is now over the top – though don't add that to our final review.

The dashboard god keeping watch over us in the taxi today is a luminous green plastic four-inch-high statue of Ganesh.

Turning and looking behind me through the rear window, I see the entire complement of staff has come out to wave goodbye. I'm not sure if we were the only guests left, but suspect we were – we had seen no one else at breakfast.

Bouncing over rocks and avoiding craters before we reach the main road, the driver's phone started reverberating in the holder on the dashboard next to Ganesh. An instantly annoying interruption. Why do people choose such ringtones? The kind to grate on your teeth, like squeaky chalk against a blackboard or one of those cheesy adverts for car insurance you can't help but sing along with, and then can't get the tune out of your mind.

Our 'Audley' taxi driver never answered his phone once. Seems a better class of phone manners they have – I bet their ringtones are a lullaby or mindfulness music. No sooner had the driver answered it, than it rang again. It's going to be a long journey. For the next five hours, it incessantly tormented us. First the toothache tone, followed by a stream of Malayalam interspersed with the words 'virus,' and 'Allo' as the signal was lost. Again. And Again. We sat just waiting for it to call, and we were not disappointed for long. Even Ganesh started looked annoyed.

Leaving Munnar town, the dilapidated buildings and fumes choking and clouding behind us, the road opens up to expansive views under an enormous blue sky. Verdant green, the hillside tea plantations fill every direction. Dotted among narrow rows between the bushes, we catch sight of occasional tea pickers obvious by their radiant coloured clothes – reds, blues, and purples – standing out against the living richer greens of tea bushes.

Three tea pickers are taking a rest at the roadside. They catch my eye. I ask the driver to stop so I can take a photograph. From here, looking past them and down the valley, Munnar is far in the distance. Chokarmudy, one of South India's highest peaks, now fills the view. Today we are heading towards the Lockhart Valley. With connections to Scottish roots, the Harrison Malayalam plantations began here in 1879. Spoiled for choice for tea factories to visit, we decide on the Lockhart Tea Factory and museum sitting on the slopes of Chokarmudy.

It's easy to know we have arrived. It's not the arch we walk under from the car park declaring in large blue letters – The Lockhart Tea Factory – more it's the rich, earthy, and smokey smell of tea emanating from multitudes of open windows. It drifts and undulates on warm breezes greeting us this high in the hills. Built of stone, the ground floor looks solid and sure. They constructed three further floors from narrow corrugated metal sheets and windows. I stand back, observing the building. It is mostly windows. Each opening is three windowpanes wide. Hundreds of open windows, all hinged on the left-hand side, are releasing waves of aroma from oceans of tea being transformed from the green leaves picked off acres of tea bushes we see in every direction. Here they process the fresh leaves into the white, green, black, and dust tea they send across the world.

A large sign proclaims the next tour is twenty minutes' wait. We stroll towards a museum. The few tourists around us, mostly nationals, are all wearing face masks. This is somewhat alarming. Are we missing something? Even more ominous are the eyes peeping behind them, scowling at the two white tourists without masks.

The small museum is a quirky, ramshackle collection of artefacts and old photographs housed in a large tin shed. I enjoy a good museum visit, meandering among glass cases, reading the details of each item, and was unsure we would have enough time to get the best of it before having to join the tea tour.

As soon as we got through the door, my concerns drifted away like steam evaporating from of a cup of PG Tips – in twenty minutes we could visit the museum four times.

I try gazing at a few photos stuck on the wall. They were out of focus. Like enlarging a Polaroid snap to the size of a poster, they had become so pixelated you could hardly see what it was. No amount of staring Magic Eye picture style would have resulted in any hidden images appearing. Next, in a glass case, sat a rusting electric fan, a glass inkpot, and a brush shoe cleaner. As if to make the point even more so, a typed simple label said – Electric Fan, Inkpot and Shoe Cleaner, helping me understand what each item was. A single black and white photo was the only item evoking any history of the place. Before the train track reached the factory, bullocks would pull carts full of processed tea down to Munnar. The convoy of these looked an impressive sight. The weirdest item on display was odd parts of an old X-ray machine used by the tea company hospital. This had an essay of a label. No matter how I tried to read the sign, the translated English made no sense.

Leaving the museum, we had time to spare – lots of time. Seeing a queue forming, and people donning blue plastic shoe covers, we join them. I'm wondering if there's any way I can turn a blue plastic shoe cover into a face mask.

Our guide to the intricacies of tea manufacturing was a distinguished-looking elder of a gentleman, smartly dressed, and seeming to engender a commanding enjoyment from the status of his position. He reminded me a bit of Omar Sharif, that mysterious, rugged look, with a splendid moustache to match. 'Follow me close,' he said, his voice distorting and echoing through a handheld PA system as the mic, pushed far too close to his mouth, was suffocated by facial hair. 'You can look, but no touch.' Repeating the phrase for emphasis, more than a few too many times. The taxi driver's ringtone started to sound good in my head. 'You can look, but no touch,' each repetition louder and more distorted until he sounded more like Darth Vader with a sore throat than Omar Sharif.

The next half hour was mildly engaging. Depending on the height of new stems, the leaves form white, green, black, or dust tea. (An Indian favourite – like the coffee perhaps?) We walked as close as we could to Omar guiding us from process to process – withering, rolling, fermentation, drying, sorting, and packing, 'Looking but no touching.' Whenever someone says, 'don't,' it always makes me more tempted to 'do.' So when Omar was looking the other way, I grabbed a few twigs. I'm not quite sure now what to do with them. I find a suitable table and dispose of them underneath.

The working conditions in some sections were grim – burning hot, humid as a steam room or otherwise chokingly dusty. It was revealing seeing what happens for me to get a cup of tea back home. Typically, my curiosity was sated more by what was beyond the boundaries of the tour. I was more interested in the warning signs nailed to walls everywhere, even what to do with a snakebite. Do snakes come inside here? I certainly would 'Look but no touching' there!'

Reminiscent of a Disneyland ride, we exit through the gift shop. We get back in the taxi with a packet of white tea, the highest quality tea you can get only picked, processed, and packed a few days before – now that's my kind of souvenir.

The miles go slow. Our driver is reluctant to change gear, the car juddering as the road is too steep for fourth or even third gear. Even Ganesh is getting frustrated. My foot keeps looking for the clutch. The scenery stays much the same. Green hills and valleys, roadside shacks selling anything and everything – temples and ornate statues of Catholic churches dominating the small villages we pass through.

The ringtone grinds again and again, 'Eh, eh, allo, allo, allo'? The mobile reception not good this high up; it cuts calls off and the ringtone blares again and again and again. My teeth are tiring. Relieved, we descend into Amaravathi, Thekkady. Our driver does not know where he is going. Wanting this journey to end, I direct him using Google Maps, happy I'd been tracking our route.

The road leading to our hotel was steep - too steep for comfort. Even our driver has to go into first gear – something achieved at the very last second before stalling. We leave tarmac at one stage, driving over rocks more suitable for a Land Rover than a small saloon. There is a last climb so uphill we hear the rear of the car scraping on the floor. Ganesh, Noreen, me, and perhaps more so the driver breathes a sigh of relief when we arrive at our hotel for tonight. The receptionist checks us in and points to a blackboard with activities for the evening. No fire dancing here. But, should we wish, we could do a spot of towel folding. Sounds too dangerous, I think we'll give that a miss.

The pictures on the website looked incredible – nothing compared to the reality of the location; it is breathtaking. The small white bungalow is on stilts set against the hillside, giving the feeling you are sleeping in the treetops. Our room is beautifully furnished like a cottage in Country Living magazine. Delicate white wicker chairs, floral cushions, and a matching sofa. Picture windows span one wall leading to a small balcony. The vista from our bed is across mountains and down into a valley. We even have a loo with a view. I'm regretting only booking one night here. We try not to trash the room too much, unpacking our swimming costumes and heading for the pool we spotted, hopeful of finding a space to catch the last sun of the day.

There was little reason to worry – most guests had deserted the hotel. We have the pool and magnificent view to ourselves. The term 'infinity pool' got its name here. Doggy paddling (my preferred swimming stroke), I flap toward the glass wall. I could swim off the side of the mountain. We catch our breaths in this moment (from the ice cold of the water) but just as much recognising our fortune and so grateful for life to give us the experience of such a place, and to ourselves – we still have not seen another guest. The 'Mary Celeste' feeling is becoming uncomfortable. We swim, read, and try to take it all in, but fail miserably. There are too many rosebuds for the gathering. We need to try again later.

Heading to dinner, like a rare bird or shy tiger, we finally spot two other 'tourist' couples. To our surprise, one we have met before. It was at our first hotel, the same Mancunian guy who suggested sending out for a beer. We are both amazed we should catch up here, miles and days away, and high in the hills from where we first met. I almost ask him, 'Are you with Audley?'

They tell us they are heading on to Chennai to meet their son and grandchildren, who now live in India.

Unperturbed by their talk of a virus spreading across the world, we leave our curtains open, watching the lights of the village opposite slowly go out, one by one.

Chapter 22

It's All Downhill from Here

Starting as a single band of greyness, and now bleeding upwards from the earth, the horizon slowly oozes shades of red and orange across the silent valley. The sky is beautifully bursting awake in all its glory. I could attempt to capture nature display the arrival of another day in Kerala with a shutter on a camera. Instead, I stand, letting it soak deep into my memory and, deeper still, into my soul.

Containing a simple table, lounger, and chair, our balcony hangs in the treetops. Opposite, appearing one by one, a few lights flicker on – life exists over the valley. The bark of a dog. The lazy crow of a cockerel echoes towards me. Drowning out these distant sounds, birdsong begins.

The trees overflow with nervous birds. An orchestra of tiny perching silhouettes begin the morning concerto. A single call crescendos into a cacophony of woops, whistles, and caws, the musicians darting to and fro in the blackness. It will never sound exactly like this ever again – a one-off performance. Standing in the beauty of it all, I'm filled with gratitude.

The village opposite is awake – dawn now fully here. Other mornings, peaceful flutes carried prayers heavenward. Today, it's a local radio station. High-pitched, repetitive rhythms, the sound nasal, not vocal, is shattering the moment. As daylight increases, with it, a thick mist is seeping in across the valley. The show is over.

It's an early start. If 'Pete's DIY Tours' had planned two nights here, it would have been a better decision. We both left, wishing we could have stayed longer.

At breakfast we meet the couple from the first hotel again. Coincidences like that amaze me. How can that happen? We chatted about the routes we had both taken; they too were independent travellers. Their next journey would be a long drive to Chennai, a large city on the East coast, to meet their family. Their son and grandchildren live there. Did they get to meet them, I wonder? Tourists were abandoning India at speed, but we didn't know that then.

Leaving the mountains and plantations of Thekkady, we are heading downhill to the coast. It's a long 75-mile drive. We need to arrive at Alappuzha by noon to board our houseboat. What we didn't quite grasp that beautiful morning, was the world beyond was descending into panic.

I feel the pressure of the rear seat belt on my chest stopping me from joining the taxi driver in the front. The downhill angle of car lets me see over his head. He is a thickset man. Solid, in his forties, I would guess. Looking for his neck, there isn't one; his head sits on bulky shoulders. Nervy, high-strung, he was impatient to leave.

Our dashboard god today is a teeny-weeny plastic statue of the Virgin Mary. She wears a blue robe with a white sash, her head slightly bowed, hands raised upwards in supplication. I point to the statue. 'Mary,' I say.''My God is Mary, and she looks after me and my family,' he replies. Our driver is a fervent believer, even calling his car 'Mary,' pointing to the sticker running along the top of the windscreen. Leaving the outskirts of the village, we pass a large Catholic church, white, cartoon-faced statues of saints filling the skyline. 'That's my church,' he says. It's neighbour is a substantial mosque, its minarets competing with the statues for the highest peaks. The proximity of religions and the synthesis of faiths is feeling unsurprising.

It's all downhill from Thekkady to Alappuzha. The road starts high in the hills, the border between Tamil Nadu and Kerala not far beyond. It hairpins down through valleys towards the coast. Tea plantations give way to fields of pineapple and rubber tree forests, the property of Boyce Rubber, billboard signs proudly declare. We drive through Vandiperiyar, 'The Land of Mist,' which earns its name, obscuring an impressive college set back from the road offering management courses, English lessons, and BAs in Travel and Tourism. Endless hairpin bends navigated at speed make me feel queasy. Deathly mangled cars at the roadside do not help. We drive by an accident. Smashed wing mirrors look the only injuries sustained. The atmosphere in the car is as thick as the mist outside.

'I need breakfast,' he tells us. We stop, and he shuffles inside the open-fronted cafe and bakery. Safety in numbers. Together Noreen and I head towards the basement toilet. Even the toilets are downhill. A fear before travelling to India was stoop 'hole in the ground' toilets. The toilets, or 'sanitarys' as they call them, are not holes, more like back home. We pass shops 'piling them high and selling them cheap' lining them up outside like seats in an auditorium just waiting for the audience to arrive. This one could have been worse – only just.

The journey lagged, mountain vistas changing to faceless towns. We reach Changanassery, a bustling city. Checking the Google map on my phone, I see we are still fifty minutes away from the bridge at Alappuzha where we board the houseboat. The landscape flattens out, canals and paddy fields expanding both sides of the road. On a racetrack, they would call this the straight. The Romans could have built it. For no reason, the driver floors the accelerator, overtaking at speed seeming mandatory, regardless of what was heading directly at us. This becomes the most terrifying experience of driving on our journey. Before we left for India, I read through guidelines on the government website for travellers. Wise, but not an engaging read. The biggest cause of injury and death for tourists was road accidents. I understand why.

Our driver turns his head and says, 'I have a terrible headache, do you have any pills?' I'm not surprised – I'd had one too and I wasn't driving. We pass a sleeve of strong painkillers forward. Both hands off the steering wheel, he presses them out then, unscrewing the bottle of water held between his knees, glugs them down. It became obvious he didn't know where he was going. One-handed, he taps the digits I give him into his phone. The last minutes of the journey were agony. I'm sure I see Mary breathing a sigh of relief when we pull up outside a secure compound.

Getting out of the taxi I didn't quite bend down and kiss the earth, but standing on solid ground prompted generosity. I hand over our fare and a tip. Glancing at me, he examined the wads of notes in his hand. 'Don't you have any new notes?' he says. Unaware the money I had given him was old notes, I shake my head. The tip I had given was almost a day's rate of pay.

Holding the cash with disdain, and with an eventual mumbled 'thank you,' he crams the notes in the back compartment of his wallet. I wished I hadn't bothered. As the driver sulked away, I offer a positive, 'Hope you head gets better.' 'It will be after I get some lunch,' then added, 'if I can with these old notes.'

Two men emerge, take our cases out of the boot and disappear at speed. Our bags now out of sight, I wanted to follow them just as quick; I wave goodbye to the driver's back as the gates clank shut behind us.

Chapter 23

Messing About on The River

A ROW OF FOUR red plastic chairs sat patient along one wall, queuing towards a dark green glass panelled door. The reception office was a small square room, but the scene more like a corridor outside the headteacher's office. Relieved, I see our two cases. We took the furthest seats away from the entrance, closest to an air-conditioning unit. Opposite us leaned a rickety desk. On it, skyscraper towers of paperwork somehow balanced; one brief blast of air would collapse years of book-keeping. But there was no air in the room. Even the walls were sweating.

The authoritative door in the corner was ajar. It yawned open enough to reveal someone important doing something important on an important-looking desk. As the door gapped open further a second time, like a sniffer dog catching contraband at an airport, Noreen spotted the green bottle of white wine on the desk – that was enough. A task was delegated. My role is to ask if they sell drinks onboard the houseboat. Another couple entered following their cases and sat on the remaining chairs.

A young man appeared from behind the stacks of paperwork to complete our booking information, handwritten in triplicate, handing us one and balancing the copies on the stacks of administration. Then he beckons the group of four with one finger to look at a small map on the wall.

It is the size of a large postcard. We have to stand too close for comfort – the term 'social distancing' hadn't been invented yet. If it had, this would not be it. The man explains with the same finger where our houseboat will take us over the next twenty-four hours. I sit down, none the wiser. I am getting concerned by the use of 'you.' Disconcerting, it began sounding like the closeness of the map reading could continue on to the houseboat. I dig through my paperwork to find the booking form stating it was only 'us' and not 'you' on the houseboat. I'm feeling slightly relieved when the important person who sat behind the important-looking door, at the important desk with the white wine on it, came out and greeted us. Suave, charming, and polite, the tall important man greets us as 'The Manager.'

He speaks perfect English, but with an undistinguishable accent. It had the aroma of public schools, rowing at Henley Regatta or doing a grand tour of Europe in the Summer. Within three of four sentences, he wishes us all a pleasant trip. The well-worn speech for the new guests complete, he lets the green door close behind him without me getting the chance to ask about the bottle. Out of the corner of my eye, I spot our cases on the move again. They are being carried out along across the jetty and across a narrow gangplank and onto a houseboat.

Moored bow-on to a jetty are six houseboats called Kettuvallams. The lower sections of the boat are wood harvested from jackfruit trees, the upper hand stitched with coconut ropes called coir. The original Kettuvallams were haulage boats. While these houseboats may look traditional, with air-conditioned bedrooms, super comfortable living areas and viewing decks, they are a floating luxury hotel room, perfectly designed for the backwaters of Kerala. Our home for the next twenty-four hours. It is only 'us' after all. Us and our crew, that is. Our crew comprised three men waiting at attention to greet us. Vilasa, the chef, dressed in his kitchen whites, the other two crew dressed in monogrammed polo shirts. This will be the most expensive night of our India stay and one of the planed 'peaks' of the trip.

The engine chugged and throbbed into life. Reversing from the jetty, we join the gallop of houseboats heading away from the boatyard. Feeling like we were in the middle of the starting line of the Grand National, Kettuvallams of all sizes were vying for position. Our helmsman was not interested in taking the lead. He aimed for the centre line of the canal, not intimidated by the runners coming up on the inside. 'Booze Cruise' was gaining position, a nose ahead of 'Audley Special,' while 'Dignified Abroad' was making ground. Steady, sure, and unperturbed as the other boat's speed past, he kept a straight line. The race spread out along the backwaters and we settled into the journey.

Behind the ship's wheel, on the deck, were four large cushions spread out like loungers and behind them two cane armchairs and a small dining table. Benches with more cushions snuggled up along the edges of the houseboat. The Kettuvallam sides were open, but neatly stashed tarpaulin blinds were rolled up under the coconut rope roof. On this boat were two bedrooms. The room we chose had an enormous bed made up beautifully, towels folded neatly on the end and a teak panelled bathroom with a shower. The room was as pleasingly chilled as a good bottle of white wine. The Kettuvallams sit low in the water. Looking through our bedroom window the surface of the backwaters were almost within touching distance. Towards the rear of the boat was a galley and, I'm guessing, most likely where the crew sleep. At the stern, hanging off the back looking like an afterthought, is a large noisy transformer, powering the AC in the bedroom.

Room now fully trashed by opening cases, we head to the reclining chairs where two coconuts are waiting for us on a small table. They look appealing, the top sliced off with red and yellow straws sticking out. Warm, pure coconut water tastes like the dregs from last night's washing up looks. Try everything once, someone told me. Not a bad adage, but along with Morris Dancing, I'd leave fresh coconut juice off that list.

It wasn't like this for Joanna Lumley. I watched her India tour on TV. She spent time on a houseboat, so I'm following in her footsteps – but not her scarf. She is unequivocally a woman who can wear a scarf well. On filming day, they must have cleared the backwaters of traffic for her. Not for us – the M25 at rush hour is quieter, several boats still vying for position on the canal.

At the water's edge, a man surfaces, washing shampoo off his head and now applying it under his arms. A woman shouts something to him as she is washing their dinner pots not three feet away. Children somersault off a concrete jetty, shrieking with laughter. Another woman is beating her washing on stone blocks submerged at the water's side. Between them bobs the flotsam and jetsam of life – plastic water bottles, beer bottles, food scraps, and floating turds. I have no inclination whatsoever to join them in the water.

We reach Bemberad Lake. The canal opens up to broader waters as the flotilla of boats spread out and disappear from view. Above us, large flocks of red kite are circling. I was an ornithologist – once. It lasted a day. I joined the RSPB. Up at dawn, I wanted to hear and identify the morning chorus. Notebook in hand, I couldn't tell a sparrow from a blackbird or a thrush from a pigeon. So that was that. I know these are red kite, as the captain points them out, as well as the bank where we will stop for lunch.

On a snow-white tablecloth spread out before us are tandoori fish, vegetables, and rice. Running alongside the boat, children are returning from school, hopping from concrete block to concrete block on broken banks, dressed in shirts as white as the tablecloth. How, being washed in this water, is a mystery. A couple pass us by waterside in a homemade coracle, the man swinging the oar with little effort, the woman straining to bring an empty net back in the craft. During lunch we casually mention the duet of a phrase – beer and wine – with the universal hand signals of drinking to Vilasa, the chef. 'You want beer' he replies, imitating our impression of downing a beer. I nod, saying, 'Yes.' 'Yes,' he said. But what did that mean? I wander up the boat towards our room and spy the second mate fast asleep on the bare wooden floor of the second bedroom.

Lunch over, the crew cast off and we head along narrow canals, few boats in sight. This lasts for a restful couple of hours. The houseboat pivoted a sharp corner, the ship's wheel turning fast, and aims for a collection of ramshackle tin shacks on the edge of the canal.

Moored is a tourist cruise boat offering 'Beautiful River Cruises' and a rusted ferry. The cruise boat has sunk. The ferry looks doubtful if it might make the crossing to the other side. We tie up between them. A straggle of men are returning from work, tools under their arms and queuing to board the ferry, along with several women, enormous plastic shopping bags in hand.

Like a scene from a 1960s spy movie, the captain gets very close to me and, speaking behind his hand, whispers, 'You want beer and wine?' I nod. He has a large backpack in one hand and my new shiny 1000 rupee note in the other. Along with the second mate, now awake from his slumbers, they head off at speed across the field and scarper out of view around the back of the tin shack. They return even faster. They hold the backpack tight, guarding it as you would a newborn baby. With arms flailing, voices shrill, they command Vilasa to set sail. Why there was such a need for speed and secrecy with our booze? I will never know.

The Kingfishers and the Sauvignon are in the fridge, ready for dinner. The extra power from the noisy transformer working just that bit more was like a sweet lullaby sounds to a baby. We soon rejoin major waterways and meet up with the rest of the company's houseboat fleet at our overnight stop.

Organised for our afternoon entertainment is a canoe trip. Shaped from a tree trunk, and narrow, it was by my guess the width of one and half tourists, but had places for three couples to squash on three planks. The couple we met in the office climb aboard, joined by one more. He an avid photographer, she resplendent in a large, floppy sun hat with a life of its own. I was expecting at any moment to hear those words, 'Are you with Audley?' They sit us at the back behind Nikon and 'The Hat.'

The outboard motor had a long shaft and a small propeller. The driver cranked it into life. Heading away from the busy river, we join a small canal not much wider than the canoe. Water hyacinths spread out before us. The deep green leaves thrive somehow in these waters, and our canoe was gliding smooth across the verdant carpet. Where we were going, however, I couldn't see. Between the size of the telephoto lens and the width of the hat they blinded the direction, so I turned to face sidewards.

Backwater life was now being observed in the way you might visit a zoo, meandering along peering into this enclosure and that exhibit. I feel uncomfortable. Not liking being distant and observing, I would rather mingle and chat. By the expressions on faces, those staring back at me felt the same way. Few smiles here.

A short arm's length away, families were washing clothes, washing kids, and washing pots. Bamboo canes, their thin nylon line lines removed from the water as we pass, are dipping for a lucky bite. Compared to this section, the man I saw showering earlier was in crystal-clear waters. Every human waste possible was being emptied into the water as men, women, and children did routine daily activities involving water. Hair washing, teeth brushing, pot washing, rubbish emptying, then eating the fish caught for dinner.

The homes on either side were lower than the height of the water. A few ripped and half-filled sandbags, tentative and lazy, held back the dirty water. Everything behind them looking insecure, pensive, and uncertain waiting for the approaching rainy season floods. Paddy fields stretched behind and beyond these concrete shacks. Hard to find any 'small but beautiful' homes here.

Canoeing these stretches of the backwaters felt packaged and intrusive, like watching local life as a scientist might observe a mouse in a cage. I caught a slight smile or an odd casual wave from the observed, but mostly felt an overwhelming and pervading intrusion into the lives of the families who call these stretches along the banks of the backwaters home. This is not traveling for me.

Back at the houseboat, I reflect on how grateful I am for my life, and the life of my family. But for the lucky roll of the 'dice of life' that gave birth to me where it did, it could have been so different.

The two cane recliners look more inviting than the offer from the crew to join other guests for a walk across the fields. Besides, the beer and wine are cold, the evening warm and sticky, so we decline. Our crew are happy with our choice – they can stay onboard. They talk of 'The Virus' and how many guests are canceling boats; there is an air of uncertainty for them in coming days. Like a cloak of heaviness around us, the atmosphere changed somehow in that moment.

They serve dinner. Joining us are our guests for the evening – mosquitos and bugs of alarming sizes. Our meal is cooked and served with care and attention, far too much for us to eat, a fact we acknowledge as we down a few mouthfuls. Across the water from our mooring, evening prayers roll towards us from a temple, not the moment-shattering din of the morning radio blaring across a valley which now feels days, not hours and miles away, from here uphill. Gentle flutes and soft sitars drift towards us.

A family of geckos appear from behind a picture frame on the wall. Five curious creatures dart, dive, and skim the walls and ceiling, eating the other guests, superglue feet holding them wherever they want to go. We decide it is time to retire to the comfort of our air-conditioned room and bid the crew good-night, apologising for the amount of leftover food. 'No problem,' says Vilasa, 'That's our dinner.' We wish we hadn't eaten so much now.

Stored between shirts, shorts, and socks in Noreen's case were two packets of Scottish shortbread fingers. We had packed three. Emergency food rations if required, but more to give to the hosts of our homestays as a gift. It overjoyed Rupasi, relishing the buttery smell, the crumbling texture bringing back memories of her time in England. She alone would have these as a secret nighttime snack in the comfort of her bedroom, she whispered to me. Keeping one packet for the host of our last stay, there was one remaining. Now chatting in bed, the thoughts of our leftovers being supper for the crew, we agreed they might enjoy adding a few shortbread biscuits for dessert.

A few minutes of maximum AC, and the rush of heat is like opening an oven when I pull at the cabin door. The night heat rushes and clings to me. Heading towards the galley along a narrow corridor, I see a thin linen curtain is part pulled across the entrance. Sheer panic breaks out behind it. I learned no Malayalam before we came to India. It didn't matter. Garbled sentences, panicked eyes, a rush to cover three naked chests with monogrammed polo shirts translated the words. Guests must not see the crew at rest. Vilasa won the prize for the quickest chest covered. I offer him the biscuits. Surprise replaces fear in his eyes, followed by one of those waggling Indian smiles. Behind him, the crew namaste gratefully. 'Can I get coffee at seven o'clock?' I ask. 'Breakfast is at eight,' he says. Then, I think willing to agree to anything for me to leave the holy of holies, he adds, 'OK, OK, coffee at seven, no problem.'

It's six o'clock. I am wide awake.

Grabbing around in the dark, trying to be quiet, I get dressed. The heat outside the bedroom, walking onto the corridor, hit me as would a five-pound salmon swung with a force above shoulder height straight at your face.

The tarpaulin blinds rolled neatly underneath the roof during the day hung down, sealing and securing the front section of the boat. A large electric fan working at maximum velocity circulated high rolling waves of heat. It was not a dry heat like a sirocco blowing across the Sahara, but wet and humid, wafting the stale smell of curried sweat with feint overtones of Scottish shortbread towards me. I was struggling to locate the light switch. It was a blessing. Three snoring shapes on the deck would have gone cataclysmic had they awoken to discover the guests seeing them sleeping. No sneaking into the spare bedroom for them. Bed for them each night of our cruise is on the wooden deck. I return to the quiet and chill of the cabin and wait for seven o'clock.

Fresh coffee, fruit, eggs, and toast for breakfast. We watch the day begin as workers are taking ferries and schoolchildren are taking the bridges over the canals carpeted with vegetation, never taking their eyes off mobile phones. The maze of the backwaters tricked us in believing we had travelled far from the start of our journey. Not so; within an hour we would be back at the marina. The taxi will be waiting for us when we arrive, Vilasa tells us.

We arrived back at the marina far earlier than I had planned, 'Pete's DIY Tours' getting it wrong. The journey to our next stop at on the beach was an hour at the most by taxi. I worked out we would arrive well before check-in time. But I had a hunch it would be OK.

From six months before, when I wrote to Allwyn the owner of our next homestay, I was looking forward to meeting him. His emails were warm and inviting. He was interesting and interested. Along with confirmations of rooms booked, he sent photos of himself and his wife Jency enjoying religious festivals and snaps of Shanku, their cute dog. Questions always accompanied his chatty style of writing. He wanted to see photos of where I lived, and the dog I told him I had. From the boat, I email him to ask if it would be OK to arrive early. No problem, came back the instant reply. Be prepared, he added. When you get to the jetty, they will want you off the boat quick. He was right.

The major waterway was filling with returning boats, as busy as when we left. Spanning the water ahead, the bridge signalled the end of this part of the trip and the beginning of the next.

Jostling for their final mooring, three houseboats arrive together. I look across to the next houseboat and see the awkward exchange of giving a tip without making it too obvious taking place. Hidden in one hand, the notes pass in a handshake – the giver wondering if it was enough, the receiver wondering how much is now in their palm, but not looking, only nodding with gratitude. I try the same exchange on our boat a few minutes later.

Our cases are off at speed again, navigating the gangplank without a care or delay, hoisted on shoulders by one of the crew. We follow them. Allwyn was correct. From docking to getting in the taxi was only five minutes. It took us longer to pass the first hawkers we have met on our trip.

I had been expecting, and if I'm honest looking forward to, 'lookie-lookie' requests from street sellers as part of the India experience. This was the first and only. Their wares on sale – peacock feather fans, dreamcatchers, and wooden elephants – look dusty, tacky, and desperate, as forlorn as the faces of the hawkers. No sale today. The passengers from the houseboats ahead pass by, waving them away like flies off a dead animal. I was more interested in making sure we got into the same taxi as our cases.

I yell, unable to keep quiet, the observation we were driving at oncoming traffic on their side of the road passing by our driver. No deity sits on our taxi dashboard today. Strangely, it is unnerving. I wish there was some god looking over us on this journey. Incredulous, he looks at me in the rear-view mirror followed by incessant horn blaring as the bus misses us by inches. He needed no god; he was his own god – 'King of the Road.'

We pulled up outside two steel gates; a welcome arrival at our next location. Moving from city to town, to rural pastures, the journey complete, we breathe for the first time in an hour. There was a large metal handle on the gate. It was cast it in the shape of the sun, the way a child might draw the sun, a round centre with waves radiating outwards.

The sun started turning slowly, loud creaking capturing our attention. Tall and lean, with black relaxed hair, t-shirt, and shorts, a slender man appears. This is Allwyn. He pulls open the homestay gate. Later, deep in conversation together, Allwyn would open his heart to tell us the story of how love conquered all.

Chapter 24

Rosebud Conversations

After the frantic journey from Alleppey, this tranquil oasis feels safe, shielded, and secure.

About the height and a half of a tall man, a solid concrete wall borders the plot of land, at a guess, about half an acre. There is okra, pepper, mango, passion fruit, papaya, bananas, chillies, and tapioca growing around me. I feel like I'm sitting in a greenhouse in a botanical garden back home.

The room is open on three sides, the fourth attaching itself to a large single-storey concrete house with a pitched roof of faded orange and peach terracotta rectangles shaded underneath jackfruit trees.

In front of a waist-high desk, stacked high in vertical and horizontal rows, dog-eared paperbacks spill out of shelves, inviting you to take time and read while you stay here. They are the best kind of stories to read on holiday – Lee Child and Wilbur Smith type adventures. One or two weighty reads sit between the paperbacks, looking like bright kids in a classroom of mischievous layabouts.

Positioned around a low coffee table are two bench seats, with feather soft cushions covering them. The indented shapes of being sat on for many hours show this is a library often in use. It is impossible to see the surface of the table as white beaches, mountain ranges, and jungle scenes from National Geographic, Condé Nast, and other travel magazines colour the view. But overshadowing them in serious grey, a national newspaper declares the first confirmed cases of the virus in Kerala.

Allwyn matched the man I imagined him to be through his gentle and open communication in the emails. He introduced us to Jency, and Shanku – the rescued street mutt – who was now relaxing heavy on my feet. Allwyn had bright, energetic eyes, and smooth, surefooted movements toned by the yoga he does every morning at dawn. Allwyn wore a pale blue singlet tank top t-shirt, over red shorts, and well-worn flip-flops. Jency arrived with some drinks. 'How are you enjoying India?' Allwyn asked. 'It's been such an adventure, so many beautiful places, and everywhere we have been people seem to smile,' I reply. 'All those people have stories,' he says. 'Behind each smile is great sadness; we smile to hide it.' Then, looking directly at Jency, he says, 'Our story is like that.' Allwyn spoke excellent English, punctuating his speech with idioms and a rich vocabulary, eloquent and adept in his second language. 'You speak and write excellent English,' I say. 'Yes, I learned it in my childhood watching English movies with English subtitles,' he says. 'I always had the strong desire to get out of India for a brighter future. Unfortunately, I only reached Italy, where my English was worthless. So I learned Italian.'

This glimpsing revelation piqued my curiosity to know more, sensing, here was an opportunity for a rosebud conversation.

I've learned when meeting people for the first time, gathering rosebuds always follows attentive listening, not speaking. I once read a quote by Ernest Hemingway about how people don't listen. But if they did, if they listened intently, they would learn so much. He was right. It's a bugbear of mine. It's often how what I call a non-conversation goes.

A non-conversation is where I say, for example, 'Oh, did you know I'm going to Spain next year for my holidays?' And the reply is, 'I went to Spain once.'

Then the non-conversation begins.

Where what deep down what I want to hear is, 'That's interesting, where are you going in Spain?' Eventually, I know the conversation will get around to, 'Have you been to Spain?' But non-conversations are not like that.

A non-conversation is where I don't listen to hear but listen to find the opportunity where I can speak next. I'm guilty as charged sometimes.

At fifty-nine and three quarters, (maybe it takes that long) I've learned there is another kind of conversation I can have. It's these conversations that reap harvests of rosebuds. I'm grateful to another American writer, a wise bespectacled teacher, for instilling in me the art of listening with intent. By doing so, it filled the granaries of my past with rosebud conversations.

Many years ago I read How To Win Friends and Influence People by Dale Carnegie for the first time. It's not the slick sounding self-help book it sounds, but a wonderful essay on understanding human nature. I own several copies. I discovered my most treasured copy at a garage sale in America.

On a road trip in rural Indiana, USA, passing through one junction towns, I stopped at a small ranch-style home. The front 'yard' as they call them, full of boxes, bric-à-brac, and a sign – Garage Sale Today. Most of it was the dusty good intentions and remnants of a life, otherwise known as exercise equipment, smoothie makers, and food steamers, and several boxes of stuff, the kind we will never use, look at, or touch again, but is impossible to let go. So we don't. It's left for someone else to sell at a car-boot or yard sale, after we have gone.

Digging around in one box, I found a copy of Carnegie's book. Dog-eared, well-read, the handwritten notes on each page captivated me. Sections underlined with questions in the margin, the book a priceless insight into its owner's life. The owner was a US Marine stationed at a training camp to prepare for deployment to Vietnam. I know that from the notes in the front. Did he bring it back, or was it sent home? That I'll never know.

Dale Carnegie mentions in the book a time he was at a party meeting someone and, with true interest and genuine questions, listened intently. They talked together for hours. At the end of the party, the guest was telling the host how great a conversationalist Carnegie was – and he hardly said a word. He mostly listened. I would also think, though they did not describe it in the book, if you had asked Carnegie about the conversation, he would reply much the same. He left learning more about the other person as well as sharing some of his life.

Rosebud conversations are not one sided. A rosebud conversation is not a manipulation, a way to be liked. Instead, a rosebud conversation is when I seek a deeper and genuine connection through the shared experiences of life, the interests, and values we hold in common. These are the conversations where I visit places I will never see, feel experiences I will never feel, and meet people I'll never know. These are conversations where we both enjoy the telling and the listening. These are the conversations I love.

Of course, some people are not interested in those conversations. They like non-conversations. So with grace, I try to give them what they are looking for. But I can tell the conversation I am about to have will not be like that.

'Italy?' I say. 'How did you find yourself in Italy?'

Chapter 25

Love Conquers All

Allwyn and Jency grew up in the tiny village where we are staying. The narrow roads form crisscrossing lanes from the beach through the leafy green countryside until they reach the main road. They lived about a mile from each other in the village. They went to junior school at the same time, though not together.

Allwyn and Jency were the same age, separated by the segregating lines of caste – he a landowner's only son, she a fisherman's daughter. Like an invisible border, or one of those underground security lines shocking you if you cross it, the caste system separates everyone from birth.

Belonging to the higher class of 'landlords' forbade Allwyn from playing with the local kids. His father would not allow it, a line he couldn't cross. Allwyn, as I would learn, was not someone who 'coloured within lines' – invisible or not. He would play with all the kids around him anyway, only without telling his father.

Allwyn wanted to play the national sport of India – cricket – with his friends. Escaping from his house, he would soon be at the crease slamming the ball around. No matter how much fun he was having, he always knew he had to climb back over the garden wall before his father returned home. Sometimes it didn't happen. The stress was enormous in his young mind. While the injustice of it all at a young age caused fearful anxiety to be constant, it also was forging a steel will, a core of resilience within him at the same time without him knowing it.

Leaving their independent schools as mid-teenagers, Allwyn and Jency would travel together to Cochin every day to work and study. Allwyn was working in a bank sales department while Jency was continuing her education. Friendship became a relationship. Relationship grew into love. A love forbidden to cross the line. Saving money from the birth of a child, and wanting the best for their children, marriages and dowries dictate the course of love. 'It's how things happen here,' Allwyn says. 'Wealth, position, status, and control have more power than romance or affection. In India, everyone is interested in control – control of your money, who you can marry, and what you can or can't do with your life. I only learned that bitter truth having to leave India.'

'What happened, to make you leave?' I asked.

Allwyn and Jency were in love. However much the mind knows the rules, the heart does not follow its course along lines prescribed by others. But if only it were simple for some to fall in love. Allwyn and Jency wanted to be with each other, though in no doubt of the fervent opposition that would be the result.

One day Allwyn told his father he wanted to marry Jency. On the same day, Jency told her father she wanted to marry Allwyn. 'I forbid it,' both fathers responded. The opposition was not the man, but the caste – not the woman, but the position in society. The stigma, condescension, and suspicion engendered by caste rules. It wasn't even about religion; they both were Catholic in their faith. They locked Jency in her bedroom. Allwyn told they would disown him as a son if he persisted in even talking about her.

The talking stopped. But love didn't, and we know that love conquers all. They would do what lovers have done for all time; they would run away together.

A few days later, planning their escape, Allwyn gave instructions to a friend in a sealed note, passing the same message through an open window to Jency. Now what they needed was for seven o'clock to arrive. Motorbike revving at the end of the drive, Jency started running towards the sound of love and freedom with little more than the clothes on her back. They sped to Cochin and married in a Catholic church a few days later. Their first home together was the streets of the city, sleeping for the first six months in alleyways and under bridges. Jency could not go back home; her family would tell everyone that no longer did they have a daughter by that name. Banned forever from bringing 'that girl' home, Allwyn's parents wouldn't even say her name. Allwyn, faithful to his duty as a son, still sent money each month to his father.

It would be Allwyn's mother who made the first phone call. 'You can return home, but "she" cannot enter the front door. "She" can't use the kitchen when we do. "She" sleeps around the back. "She" must work in the house for no pay. "She" can't look at us, can't ever talk to us.' There was little choice. The money they had left each month after paying their families was not enough for them to live alone, so they came back to the house attached to the reception room where we are sitting.

Jency returns. I don't know how often this story is told to guests, but it feels by the look in her eyes it is rare. Her head tilts, her eyes gaze down towards the floor; we're not sure she wants the story told, but Allwyn continues.

There is a story of hope and riches told by Indian families to their children, he explained. Study hard and get a job in Dubai, America, in Europe, if you are lucky enough, England. If you do, then you and your family will be rich, retirement secured. 'Look around here,' says Allwyn, 'see the big houses between the small ones; most are families that have had children working abroad at one time. Ten to twenty years overseas, then you can return home rich – rich by the standards of most families in Kerala. Rich enough to build a mansion paid for month by month, the building materials purchased and stacked, waiting for the next stage of completion. Prosperous enough to look after the family as they age. Wealthy enough for everyone to retire when you return.'

'Hope exists in Italy for you, Allwyn,' his father told him one day. 'You must go to Italy. Your Uncle is there. We will loan you €5000 for the visa and plane tickets, and one month's living expenses. Then you are on your own. But you must still send money back each month. "She" can stay and clean and cook for us.'

And that's what happened for the next two years. Allwyn went to Rome, Jency stayed in Kerala.

Arriving there, he couldn't speak fluent English then and no Italian. He found a free class teaching basic Italian and pounded the streets looking for work. He survived eating grapes and fruit hanging from trees and drank free water. Cleaning tables, washing pots in restaurants, slowly learning the language and dutifully sending his money home. Rome turned into a move to Florence. Communication between Allwyn and Jency comprised odd phone calls and letters. Hope was hard to find in Italy.

In those intervening years, something changed – not between them; love was still conquering overall. What had changed was inside Allwyn. He did find hope in Italy, but the hope he discovered had been inside him all the time. He forged it in the days of his youth.

Allwyn's world was always more significant than the smallness of his village. Not the geographical size, but in vision and understanding. Being in Italy, he could see the restrictions on his life for what they were. Not limitations placed on him by life, but by family, by caste, by birth. You never forget the place of your birth; it holds a part of you forever, even if the memories hurt. There was love for India, for Kerala, for his home. It was a love more powerful than the hurt of the situation they were in.

Back in Kerala two years later for a visit, walking one day along the beach, Allwyn met a Scandinavian couple. They planted a seed in his mind. Where he lived was beautiful, mostly untouched by tourism. It held such opportunities. They encouraged Allwyn to consider opening a homestay for visitors who were sure to arrive at some point. You can't keep a beautiful place like here a secret forever, they told him.

Leaving the second time was a wrench for Allwyn. Leaving Jency behind to the circumstances of home was heartbreaking.

Now living in Florence, Allwyn had three jobs. The major role was caring for an older man as a live-in helper. A job with accommodation would save money on living expenses. Allwyn kept those duties to send money each month to his father, but there was some left. Enough to send secret savings to Jency for them, for their future. Eighteen long months separated them for the last time. Returning to Kerala for good, with some savings, they set about bringing hope to life.

The day after returning from Italy, Allwyn got his old job back at the bank. Jency was working in Cochin at a student recruitment agency for higher studies abroad, the family still angry at them both for spoiling the dream of the big house and secure retirement.

Allwyn could see there was nothing but wasteland surrounding the family home. He shared the dream he had with his father. Here is an opportunity to create a homestay for the tourists. His father wouldn't listen. He thought it was utter foolishness, stamping on those dreams and ideas as you would a bug under your foot. He would have nothing to do with the plan. Neither should his son.

When there is a vision burning inside you, resistance tests how much you believe in it. It can snuff out your dreams or spur you on even more. It had taken the best part of five years to get to this point, and nothing was going to stop Allwyn trying. That core of determination would support the dream until it became real, however long that took.

What is it that makes some people dream and strive to make their dreams come true? With no guarantee of success, often no plan, visionaries commit to their goal. Is that spark innate in all people, or just a few?

It can be a blessing and a curse. It takes persistence and stubbornness. It takes believing in yourself and your dream when you are the only one that believes it.

The designer James Dyson made over 5000 prototypes of his invention of a new vacuum cleaner. Years before, Edison tried 10,000 versions of the light bulb. Whatever the real numbers are, I don't know, but having persistence to keep going is an act of will over reason. To keep persisting when everything and everybody around you says it won't work. Having the tenacity never to let the dream die. This determination marks visionaries out from the crowd of people who give up at the first hurdle. Or first hundred hurdles.

After many battles and disputes, Allwyn's father wanted nothing to do with the project. Finally, he agreed to lease the land to him, convinced his son would fail. Building on the first villa could now begin. One slight problem – Allwyn had built nothing before. As I say, it was only a minor problem.

From digging the footings by hand to bricklaying, Allwyn worked every hour to build the first villa. When it was too dark to work outside, Allwyn spent the night hours learning about Facebook and online marketing. He would take photos of the villa in construction, of the beautiful beaches close by and the places to visit by tuk-tuk, posting these on his page.

To his complete surprise, he got his first booking from England online and took it. At that time there was no roof, windows, fittings, or furniture in the villa. Allwyn thought it was best to stop sending pictures to Facebook, but spent every hour available building. It would not be enough for the villa to be ready for the booking. Allwyn and Jency finished the walls with coconut matting; they didn't have time to use bricks. They had to tell the first guest to be careful, as the paint wasn't yet dry!

In the next seven years, they built a further three villas and two swimming pools.

Perhaps Allwyn found hope in Italy after all.

Not far away from the homestay, on a narrow road leading to the beach only metres away, there is another impressive home. It is a home for them. It is one of those large 'beautiful' homes you pass next to the small 'beautiful' ones. The construction had just finished, and he invited Noreen and I to see it.

Allwyn and Jancy's new home would not have looked out of place on a Tuscan hillside. The architecture with soft curves, ornate staircases, and a swimming pool that wrapped around the building like a giant letter L is a testimony that dreams really come true.

It is a statement that love really can conquer all.

Chapter 26

Mother Rapper

Handmade by Allwyn, the stone villa is our home for the next three days. Constructed with rough red stone blocks, there was one large bedroom with AC, a bathroom, and a shower. In the centre of the bathroom is an impressive trunk of a jackfruit tree stretching up and out of the ceiling missing above the shower area. You could call it a 'natural' skylight. Showering under this canopy of leaves, with the music of birdsong, will be a beautiful and memorable start to each day.

Our living area is an expansive L-shaped veranda patio stretching beyond the villa. Hanging in one corner, a deep rattan cocoon chair swings from the rafters, looking inviting. Between two white columns a rope hammock sways, looking just as inviting. Two solid armchairs, four dining chairs and a simple wooden dining table make up the rest of the furniture.

Matching the beauty and serenity of the villa, our rectangle swimming pool stretches into the garden. Eight breast stokes long, four wide, it is ice-cold. To the side of the swimming pool area are a couple of sun beds, a small table, and an umbrella for shade.

It is simple, uncluttered, rustic, and exactly what we need to relax and rest. The end of our trip is arriving far too fast. The accommodation is an excellent 'fly and flop' for this part of our Indian odyssey, all the more special now we knew the history of its origins and construction.

The midday sun is hot. No mad dogs around, as far as I can see, but there is an Englishman and his wife who decides it would be a good time to go exploring.

The homestay villa is one street back from the beach, where we are heading. A few Royal Enfields thump-thump past, the odd bicycle, and ever-present tuk-tuks are the only traffic. Opposite is a narrow path between a few buildings to the beach.

A small shop hangs at the junction of the lane and the main road. Four men sit chatting. I offer the one behind the counter a rather large denomination note for the two bottles of water and a Sprite after he fetches them from a fridge in the back. He gives me a look needing no translation. In the distance we can see the sea.

The sand on the path is burning through the soles of my shoes, and baking hot grit is washing over the side of Noreen's flip-flops. Palm trees edge our way onto the beach. It stretches unobstructed far into the distance on both sides. Only three colours fill the view – a cloudless pastel-blue sky cuts cleanly horizontal at a turquoise sea until peaks of white roll onto our feet. It's not surprising we are the only ones there. It is well over 100 degrees Fahrenheit, too hot even for unhinged dogs. We head back.

We spend the afternoon much as we spend most of the next two days – reading, swimming, dozing, and eating. Jency is a wonderful cook. Our breakfast each day comprises of large bowls of freshly chopped fruits. Bananas from the trees growing in the garden, juicy watermelon, and bitter-sweet pomegranate seeds. Following this will be spicy vegetable curry, fluffy snow-white Kerala coconut rice steamed in bamboo tubes, masala omelettes, toast, and jam along with hot black coffee and cold water washing it all down. The simplicity of it all is beautiful.

Our evening meal starts arriving about 7:00 – finishing about 7:13. Plates full of steaming fish, spices crusted and crispy on the outside, are delicate and soft on the inside. There are never-ending bowls of unknown vegetables – squishy yellow roots swirl in sauce while sage-coloured chunks swim in a rich ocean of red. A few curried prawns are curling around tomatoes and cucumber. Accompanying creamy curries zinging with spices and chilli is doughy fresh parotta – a buttery, stringy South Indian flatbread.

Shanku, the dog, sits in the shade of large green leaves next to the table. There is a trio of house cats – one whose meowing cry sounds like a small child in pain. It cries often. Just as annoying are the critters, bugs, and mosquitos. To avert this, in a small bowl, coconut husks covered in paraffin oil smoulder to hold back the hordes.

The first night we return from a walk and find its glowing embers inviting, lighting up the darkness, along with redolent incense smoking under the table. Both tactics delay the inevitable retreat to the air-conditioned sanctuary of our bedroom at some point. The second evening they smoke us out in seconds. We watch with curiosity as one young guy strikes a match into the bowl sitting next to the table. Like a genie exploding from a lamp, clouds of acrid smoke billow out, choking us. We beat a hasty retreat to the bedroom with its air-conditioning filters. I shut the doors quick before the dog and three cats have time to join us.

One joy in travel is exploring new locations, checking out the back streets. So often it is those times unexpectedly rewarding. I've gathered many a rosebud in a back street. Before arriving, I had 'walked' the main road around the villa using Google Street View, seeing a little of what surrounded our location. I'd noticed a resort hotel a mile or so along the road. I email them, seeing if they allowed non-resident guests in the hotel. The reply came quick. Yes, adding there was a bar. Decision made. I set our direction for an early evening adventure.

Standing in a line outside the homestay reception, five bikes asked us for a ride. Sizing up the most suitable, we unbolt the gates and push the bikes onto the lane.

A few yards in the opposite direction of where we should head towards the hotel, something is happening. There is cheering, clapping, and the unmistakable distortion of a voice blasting through a PA system turned up far too loud. My curiosity sensors couldn't resist investigating further. Checking Noreen was following me, I turned right instead of left, and cycling a short distance pulled to a stop outside a large Catholic church.

Reminiscent of churches flashing by through taxi windows, the ornate Catholic church sat back a distance from the road. The building split horizontally, making two distinct sections. The upper comprised three sandstone-brick arched columns, spanning the width of the building and shaped liked three podgy fingers pointing to heaven. On top of the middle finger, an immense neon cross started blinking white, then lime-green, then a shocking pink – the neon pink you see on a sign outside a hotel on the Las Vegas strip.

On the middle arch, a lifesize statue of Jesus with his hands raised high in blessing was backlit by spotlights and encased in a glass capsule. It looked like a glass lift you might see on the outside of a skyscraper in a city. I'm not sure if Jesus ascended up and down towards heaven at different times of the day, or for holy holidays, but for now he was stationary. Jesus was looking across the same sizeable, excited crowd gathering on the dusty ground as I was. The group of people was growing louder and more animated by the minute.

A brightly lit porch, with steps leading down to the forecourt, made up the lower half of the building. On the steps were a bank of black speaker cabinets, piled high on top of each other. The number of them would have been the envy of The Rolling Stones at Glastonbury, the sound coming from them even louder than a stage set there.

A diminutive nun, all in white, was inciting the crowd with evangelical fervour reminiscent of Mick performing 'I Can't Get No Satisfaction!' At one time, I'm sure I heard her say, 'Hey, Hey, Hey!' but I might have been mistaken. This was no Mother Teresa of Calcutta, more the Mother of All Rappers from Kerala. A mighty force of unbridled evangelical enthusiasm, her voice started imploring the devotees for increased participation. The crowd roared in response. I wanted to shout 'Amen, Sister,' but resisted the temptation.

Now raising her hands above her head, she started clapping in time to the repetitive chords the keyboard player was stomping out with similar passion, the crowd responding and mirroring her actions. The last time I saw anything like this was watching

Take That at Cardiff Millennium Stadium. Swelling in size and ecstasy, the crowd raises hundreds of hands towards Jesus, who has not moved up any floors in the lift outside the building just yet. I am about to get off my bike and join in. Noreen senses this. She suggests it's time to go. Reluctantly, I agree.

We pedal along the busy road, motorbikes passing within inches of us, the odd car horn blaring at us, the drivers seeing how close they can get to the back wheel until we reach the gates of the hotel. The architect must have had in mind an African safari theme designing the entrance, which seems a bit out of place here.

Standing guard, a security officer smartly dressed in a military uniform, minus a pith helmet, seemed bemused by these two tourists now waiting at the red and white striped barrier. I had the feeling he was the only one allowed to touch it. He would hit me with the short baton stick he was holding if I went anywhere near it. I tell him I had emailed with the subject line Is There A Bar Here? and I had received a positive reply. Saying nothing back, he started walking along the length of the barrier to a phone on the wall. They held it in a secure box, as it would be at a border crossing. Animated, his conversation lasts much longer than the 'Can I let these two chancers in?' I thought it would be. Replacing the receiver and again walking the full length of the barrier, he lifted it by hand, letting us through. I couldn't understand why an architect had spent so much time building a replica of a hotel in Kenya and not planning for the handle of the barrier to be at the same end as the phone?

The hotel was empty. Not only of people, but of any atmosphere. I wished we had stayed to watch the spectacle developing down the road at the church. We rest our bikes against a tree, padlocking them together, and walk hesitantly into the reception area. I don't know why we imagined anyone would steal them. Not with the security on the gate and the desolation of people around.

The only person in reception was a young man sitting behind a desk designed for people standing up. I communicate to the top of his head from the nose up. I saw one hotel guest hurrying past us, but apart from that, the scene was like the dining room on the Mary Celeste. The top of his head was saying nothing. Then, like a scene from the Biblical King Belshazzar's banquet, a single finger appeared and started pointing at a sign on the wall. There is an arrow and the word 'Bar.'

Walking along narrow paths in the sparse gardens, the arrows were pointing to a small square building. Jungle safari in style, it had a thatched roof surrounded by palm trees on all sides. They set it on its own island. It wouldn't have looked out of place on the set of Born Free.

A narrow moat separated it from the land with a small gated bridge to cross over. This was no chasm. A child of two taking a gentle bunny hop without a runup could have cleared the gap with room to spare. Music was blaring inside the building. The Bee Gees were giving everything to night fever. Thinking I was hearing things, and imaging it was where all the people were, pulling hard on the fake log door, we enter inside.

We enter a refrigerated room. It could have been a morgue for all the life in there. Our evening drink was not boding well.

Set around were four small circular tables, two chairs at each, all empty. By now I was expecting to see animal heads on the walls. Instead, a large TV was blasting Western music. The Bee Gees had finished, and Robbie Williams now taking their place.

Either there had been a run on drinks, or few people came here. I am convinced it was the latter. The top shelf comprised four bottles – one of each – gin, brandy, whiskey, and vodka. There was no reason the young barman needed to ask me, 'What kind?' when I ordered a gin and tonic and a white wine. Bringing them over with a bowl of salted peanuts, he asks, 'Where are you from?' 'England,' I say.'London?' he says, more of a statement than a question. I explained the geography of where we live by saying, 'If you took a map of England and put a pin in the middle, that's about where we live.' 'So, Manchester,' he says.I nod yes, now realising that his English comprises cities and football teams. I was wondering if he hadn't spoken to anyone since his shift began.

We try to have a conversation. Robbie is hogging the limelight. 'Let me entertain you?' Not tonight, thanks Robbie. Nibbling on the nuts in the bowl, our barman went back to restock the shelf.

Putting the one bottle of gin back, we see another barman walk in through a side door. This barman is pushing a sack trolley of empty beer crates five high. He then refills them in the storeroom from the clanging and crashing offstage we hear. Beers replenished, he heads off in a rush – to where? I want to follow him to where all the people must be. But if our experience of buying beer on this trip has taught me anything, there is a more likely a queue of locals lined up outside the gates waiting thirsty for his return.

'This is going to be expensive,' Noreen warns. She was spot-on. I balked, asking him to repeat the amount when he gives me the receipt. It was about £17 for two drinks. I understand why the bar is empty. Robbie Williams, Noreen and I, and our barman pass the time counting goosebumps on our arms. By the time we left, the nut bowl was empty, but the granaries had another rosebud or two.

Seated on the patio of our villa, we hear Mother Rapper in full flow. Sounding as if she and her keyboard player were on the other side of the garden wall, it's hard to believe she was at least half a mile away from our homestay.

Her fervour was intense. The music sounding loud, storming on the evening breeze towards us. Still chanting, but with perhaps more urgency than three hours ago when we (well, I) found it as captivating to listen to as the crowds she transfixed by her presence. I hadn't a clue what she was saying, or the words to the songs, but I could do the actions.

Have they been listening to her all that time? Will they ever get to verse two of the hymn? Are the keyboard player's fingers bleeding? Has Jesus ascended any floors up the building by now? These were all questions I wanted answering before I went to sleep.

Allwyn returns to check if our meal was OK and did we need any more? 'Yes, and no, thank you,' I say. 'How often does this happen?' I ask, pointing over the wall towards the church. 'Every week, for a couple of nights.' The look on his face confirmed he was not a devotee of Mother Rapper. He says, 'They require the volume to be lower since I complained to the council. It has to be under 100 decibels by the time it reaches here, but it never is.' I find out a normal conversation is about 60 dB, a powerful lawn mower 90 dB, Mick Jagger and The Rolling Stones at Glastonbury 120 db. My guess earlier was correct. Her sound system would have impressed Mick and The Stones. She was peaking 100 dB from half a mile away. We head indoors.

The room is cool with the air conditioning working full blast. We drift off to sleep in the early hours, Mother Rapper not saying the final benediction till around midnight. I don't think I have the stamina to be her new convert. I've had enough 'Hey, Hey, and Hey' for one night.

Chapter 27

Fishing at Dawn

Apart from the day you are departing for home, 'being on holiday' and 'alarm clock' should not be in the same sentence.

A buzzing fills my ears. I pour boiling water on brown dust in the bottom of a cup. It was not the best day to decide to watch the local fishermen bringing in the day's catch at first light. The incessant drumbeat from Mother Rapper got into my brain, keeping me awake. Struggling to be enthusiastic, but not wanting to miss the spectacle, we saddle up the bikes and head for the beach.

Biking past the safari hotel, we turn down a narrow lane towards the sea. There is salt in the air's dampness – I can taste it as my breathing speeds up, even though the new tarmac made for easy pedalling.

We pass an old man, bare-chested, grey-white dhoti pulled up high. He is filling oversized water cans from a communal tap, then strapping them to a moped, older than him by the look of the rust holding it together. The road ends at palm trees and twists into sand. Between the trees, a few bright blue fishing boats are resting high off the ground on round sleepers. Piled next to them, heaps of nylon fishing nets look idle, like workers waiting for instructions, not willing to be proactive in the task.

The beach is quiet. We are too late, or in the wrong place. I had seen photos of smiling faced fishermen hauling bursting nets out of the sea. My collection of photos of our trip was looking sparse in the possibility of adding similar scenes. I'm now thinking getting Noreen out of bed to see this emptiness was not a good idea. As ever, I was optimistic for more.

The orb of the sun rises behind us, cascading its light between the coconut palm trees in ingots of gold. In the shadows through the solid trunks, we see two fishermen working under the canopy of shade. If what we heard earlier about the caste system still lives on here, this dawn toil has been their life since they were old enough to haul a net.

We walk closer and see the grind of the years shows on their faces, their skin hardened by sun and salt, their clothes worn through. We watch as they drag a bundle of nylon fishing net over a wooden contraption that looks suitable for a Shetland pony to use as a showjumping fence. As they do, they pick out small fish that flap for life on blue sheets of tarpaulin beneath. I've seen bigger minnows in the park pond. Passing over the low beam, the net empties its meagre catch and they gather it in. They smile at us, waggling heads side to side as we get closer. Do their smiles hide sadness too, I wonder? I motion to them the size of the fish being small. They seem happy with their catch. Looking into the remaining bundle of blue nylon, by the time they have emptied the net they might be lucky to fill a small bucket. It looks a poor catch to me. But what do I know?

At the point where the palm trees end, and the open beach started, stood a simple white wooden cross. A garland of marigolds is hanging from the crossbeam. Not dictated by religion, Christians, Hindus, and Muslims form the layers of this community. I wonder if they pray to any god before the cross for safety setting out to sea?

Our long shadows walk before us, the sun getting higher. It is one of those mornings that speak to my soul, a rosebud morning. These moments are why I travel. The rhythm of the waves reaching the shore is the only sound that interrupts the peace of the dawn. These mornings I will remember forever gathered deep away. As I write these words, I know that is true. Closing my eyes now, I am there again. The sound of the sea, the wisp of salt on the breeze, the beauty of the moment.

Walking further onto the deserted beach, looking back through the treeline, we see a few odd groups of men unloading their nets in similar ways further down the beach. We have missed the boat, in this case literally, I'm thinking. Long, narrow, brightly painted fishing boats are resting on the surrounding sand. They have deep blue hulls, rainbow stripes painted along the sides and small masts fore and aft where pink pendants hang barely moving.

A pack of stray dogs are sleeping in the sand, the same way a group of huskies might sleep in snow. Through one eye, a mutt is checking us out. His ginger flecked brown coat catching the sun, he stands up. He digs his hole a little deeper, circling three or four times, and goes back to sleep. Like him, we think there is little activity worth watching this morning. Better to enjoy the peace and serenity looking out to sea from the sand. We walk to the edge of the sea, where a steep sand bar forms a natural place to sit and gaze out across the Arabian Sea.

On the horizon, specks of black are appearing, heading towards the shore. Out quite a distance still, a small flotilla of rafts is returning. Black, and homemade by the look of them, they resemble Indian Jutti shoes, the way the front of these little inflatables turn upwards toward a point. There is enough room for one fisherman, and the large blue nylon net sitting behind him.

Paddling with what resembles a broom handle and table tennis bats at either end, the first raft hangs back, waiting for the right wave to break so he can surf onto the shore. The bright yellow of his shirt contrasts sharp against the black of the raft he is steering with ease, a mound of blue fishing net behind him. Catching the right wave, he surfs in as far as possible. Then, using the last momentum from the wave, he jumps off, pulling the craft through the shallows to a sudden stop. The sand bar breaks any more movement.

Three of the men from under the canopy of palm trees have now arrived, helping pull the raft further onto the beach. They push a large pole through rope rings on the front and, with one at each end, two men haul the raft away from the waves, the other two pulling on ropes at the back. By the effort they are exerting, the weight is obvious as four struggle to drag the craft away from the waves.

The sand is soft and deep, and the boat is heavy. Dragging it inland, it leaves a smooth path, ironing the creases out of the beach. A mutt nearly gets pressed but is too lazy to move as the raft passes inches from its nose.

Supporting the net on their shoulders, two of the fishermen carry the catch towards the trees. The other two upend the raft, the curled bow resting on the paddle. They give no instructions.

Each team is perfectly in sync. As far as we can see along the shore, the same scene repeats. The empty beach now busy, dotted black with rafts, finished with for the day and drying in the sun. The same as they have done for decades.

Larger fishing boats start arriving. They needed to catch the biggest waves to surf the boat as far as possible into the shallows. Painted in two broad stripes of turquoise blue and neon pink, the first boat makes land. One man stands steering a long oar while the rest of the crew jump out and heave. Seventeen fishermen head out from the palm trees towards the shore. A few are carrying the round sleepers we saw stacked by the nets under the canopy of palms. One has a large jerry can; it looks heavy in his hands by the way he clinches it to his chest. The boat ground itself hard on sand, as far inland as the helping hands of the sea would freely offer. Now unpaid humans needed to take over. Like a team of tyre mechanics around an F1 car at a pit stop, another well-rehearsed routine begins.

Placing sleepers at intervals up the sand bar, coconut oil from the jerry can splashes over them. A lone voice sings out above the sound of the waves. It is strong and proud, deep and smooth. In unison, the team echoes the call. The song repeats three or four times, building until on one distinct crescendo call they push the vessel up and over the sand bar, on over the steep rise, reminiscent of scenes I've seen of cotton pickers lamenting spirituals.

Were these songs of the sea with verses about their slavery? A different kind, maybe? Slaves to the circumstances of birth? On it went – call and reply, call and reply – inching forward the vessel on each cry. The sea joined in, heavy waves breaking in accompaniment. Call and reply.

When the bow reached the next sleeper, those at the front would race to the back and carry on the task, pushing the hull forward and higher onto the beach. As quick as a sleeper appeared at the stern, it would come racing back to the front to ease the boat ever forward over sand.

As the team were gaining momentum, the sound of singing became continuous. The call and reply gone, the act of singing was in perfect unison with the effort of the movement. Finally, cresting the sand bar, the boat crashed down on the sand. Now the song picked up speed and rhythm, the sweet harmony pushing the boat further onto the sand with apparent ease compared to the Everest effort needed to move the boat the first twenty or thirty feet. On and on they pushed. The coordinated teamwork practised each day made ease of the process, but I doubt it got any easier seeing the effort required.

Along the beach, five more boats had reached the sand bar, queued, waiting, ready. Occupation, caste, and perhaps faith joined the men, but friendship and camaraderie more. They were laughing, singing, whistling, and teasing each other. It was a signal for the stray dogs to get up – breakfast had arrived. Curled up balls of mangy haired strays, tails wagging, followed the boats across the sand until they reached the treeline. We followed them as well.

The long simple boat held three crossboards for sitting on. In between them, mounds of the same blue nets we saw in the trees had a few silver fish flapping in, again looking slim reward for the gargantuan effort. I wasn't optimistic for the dog's snack.

Two of the fishermen wearing straw conical hats, the sun now feeling hotter by the minute, pulled the net over the side of the boat. As they did, the odd fish dropped onto plastic tarpaulin sheets spread out below. The dog's patience was rewarded, as now and then a minnow was tossed their way. The fishermen knew the dogs, and the dogs knew them. A ruffle of the ears and stroke of the head, then another flapping fish gratefully received with the wag of a tail. A quick dash in and they could have had a mouthful. I would imagine it was a relationship of trust. It was this way each morning, the same as it had been for the years before. If these were the wildest stray dogs we came across, my fears and pains over rabies were unfounded. These were as tame as a poodle in a retirement home.

A couple of rubber buckets were being filled with small fish. There were one or two that looked enough for a meal on their own, but few. The fishermen started bartering over the buckets with a man who had arrived on cue, his tuk-tuk still running, its incessant whine breaking the peace of the morning. An animated conversation lasted seconds and cash changed hands, the fish now heading to market to be sold for ten times the price. The transaction no doubt weighted against the workers.

The life of a fisherman is financially poor, constrained by caste, dependent on the day's catch. It made me think of the conversations with Allwyn about falling in love with a fisherman's daughter. The work looked hard and unrelenting, the men just the same. Weathered by the sun and salt, dependent on the whims of nature and the kindness of the seas, these were the days of their lives. Lives like mine. Lives raising a family, making a living, living a life that passes one day at a time. Till it ends.

I didn't need to travel to India to find rosebuds. They are all around me at home; they're waiting for me every day at the end of the bridle path 20 minutes' walk away, they are new and fresh every morning. These men have no need to travel far to find rosebuds. Rosebuds are individual, not dictated by wealth or position, age or location. That's the thing about rosebuds – one man's minnow is another's meal.

There seemed one powerful force sustaining the men – they stood next to someone just like them. Someone maybe who had a daughter who could have fallen in love with a landowner's son. Someone who would turn from working their own nets and walk to the sea, hauling another's their catch over the sand. Someone who prayed to the same god. Not a god of religion, but petitioning the gods of the winds and the waves this day there would enough fish to sell, enough to eat and a few for the faithful dogs who would greet them back from the waves each day on the sands.

We were the only tourists on the beach. I wonder, what do these men think looking at us? Clean clothes, taking pictures on an expensive camera. They smile as everyone does here. Are they smiles with sad stories behind the eyes? Do they think of us as different people, with a different life? Travelling makes me grateful. Grateful to be gathering rosebuds in Kerala and just as grateful for the life I have back home.

By the circumstances of birth alone, I can choose, to a certain degree, the life I live. Of course, there are restrictions, but by effort, creativity, persistence, and perhaps a bit of luck thrown in, I've experienced a good life. Not everything that has happened has been good, and some of that is my doing. Wrong choices made. But by the circumstance of their birth, this is, and will be, their life.

I watch as a young boy in his early teens heaves his shoulders against the back of a boat. He hauls and sings the same song. What other songs could he sing, if given the choice and chance?

For the cosmic throw of the dice, and the grace of God, it could have been my life. But it wasn't and it isn't. Makes me grateful and thankful for my life even more.

It was time to leave. Our shadows much shorter now, the sun was hot on our backs.

I wish I knew the words to the song they were singing as they pushed and pulled the boats up and over the sand bar, its rhythm uniting them as one. The call and response stays on the breeze as other boats are arriving. How old is that song? I doubt much has changed along this stretch of the coast for centuries.

As we get up to leave, next to us a fisherman holds a water snake by its tail. It was thin, about three feet long and hanging like the pendulum of a broken clock, still and unmoving, as if dead. Walking down to the edge of the sea, he tossed it in the waves. Like Aaron's staff, the miracle brought it to life. Its head poking up over the surf like a periscope of a submarine, it swims out to sea. That did it. I had considered having a quick swim. Not now. We find our bikes and pedal back for breakfast.

Chapter 28

The Object of Attention

There is a significant advantage to an early morning call – the dawn adventure made the rest of the day long.

Relaxing the morning and lunch away, by early afternoon the day was cooling. I was restless. I used to think, 'When I come back here again I will do …' but at fifty-nine and three quarters, I know I won't. So I need to do it now. There are adventures awaiting beyond the gate with the sun-shaped handle. It's time to move. I'm curious to see today what the locals see every day.

Stopping pedalling, we lean the bikes against the window of a local store at a busy crossroads. We become the object of attention. A moped creeps past us, the pillion passenger sitting sidesaddle. She has a week's shopping balancing on her knees. The distance growing between us, she waves, but the smile stays.

The crossroads was more than a junction where traffic decided which way to head; it was the place locally to discuss and debate the world. Opposite is a small group of men. A few sit on red plastic chairs in the shade, some staring into mobile phones, others animated in conversation. One or two are standing, arms folded, watching nothing happening on the other side of the junction. They wrap and unwrap the dhotis around their waists. Untie, swing open, tie up, open, close, tie up, open, and close. Here in countryside Kerala, men seemingly waiting around on corners doing nothing had become a normal sight.

I see three identical posters pasted haphazardly on a roadside steel storage locker. Jesus, dressed in a bright pink robe, is standing central on the poster. Angelic rays set against a clear blue sky are radiating from behind his head. Flaxen blond hair falls around his shoulders, his skin white, his faint ginger beard neatly trimmed. Alongside Jesus is an image of a church not too dissimilar to the three pudgy fingers pointing heavenwards where Mother Rapper held her crusade two nights before. What was more ominous – although I can't read Malayalam, I didn't need to – is today's date. Our last quiet evening sitting by the pool eating dinner was fading quickly.

We take the road signposting the beach. At the entrance, nailed to a palm tree, is a wooden shrine holding a glass-fronted altar. Inside, standing behind Mary and Jesus, is a statue of a young boy. Ivory wax, mixed with pink, drips like stalactites from three candles burning beneath the statues. Sprigs of fuchsia bougainvillea colour the offerings made today.

We saunter onto the beach, where four or five makeshift stalls are selling dismal plastic balls, buckets, and spades. A stall offered food for sale from large glass jars. The items inside looked like what you see soaking in formaldehyde at a natural history exhibit, not in the least appetising. The place felt sad, as if something was missing, but I didn't know what. It was not a place to stay for long.

Fixed gear bikes are easy to ride on flat roads. We speed along even though it is hot and humid. We reach another crossroads. There is a small stall where rusty bikes spill onto the road. It is a graveyard for Atlas cycles. Piled up on the floor in a heap, brake levers are pointing skyward like rusting fingers in a desert of dry bones. Leather saddles split open, rear carrying racks are lying mangled and twisted. I'm not sure if they are scrap, or if they are probably for sale.

A short distance down a lane, we see the head and shoulders of a black statue towering over the road. Shiva's head must be 30 or 40 feet in height. His unblinking eyes are the size of a cartwheel. Hooped earrings a similar size hang slate grey and still. Coiled around his neck, a cobra ready to strike stands guard. Fierce-looking warriors too are guarding the entrance to the Hindu temple. Drifting back with us, as we head to the homestay is the smell of incense and oil lamps.

It is these random explorations of places we have travelled I often remember. Places where the object of my attention is nothing in particular. Just whatever there might be. Rewarding me, sometimes, with a unique insight into life, other times I've ended up exploring back alleys – literally. I like times when I am travelling just wandering and wondering what life is like lived here.

Across several countries, I've been fortunate to see, even briefly, life lived. Day-to-day life, raising a family, making a living, building a life. Life is much the same the world over. Eating with locals in the back streets of Florence, drinking tea in Istanbul souks, a fishing village in Croatia where the fish caught becomes a meal later shared with a family, and mountain villages in Vietnam where the pet pig greets you. The object of my attention being whatever I see, I've learned home truly is where you find it. Home is where you plant rosebuds for the future. And it's not the home what matters most, it's the people you share that home and your life with.

Chapter 29

Excellence Matters

The unmistakable rhythms, shrill voices, and percussive sounds of Bollywood music blast from a radio the size of a large matchbox hanging off the handlebars, resonating roughly with a coin-sized speaker. The distortion matches the clanking buzz of the tuk-tuk engine. We leave quiet narrow lanes surrounding the homestay and join the busy main road travelling North-South parallel to the coast. We're off on a day trip.

I always smile they call Birmingham, UK the 'Venice of the North,' notwithstanding the canals; the image in reality is not the same as arriving along The Grand Canal. We are heading to Alappuzha – the 'Venice of the East' – to go shopping. On the list is fabric. Noreen can never have enough fabric. She thinks umbrellas would make excellent gifts for family and friends back home. I will be glad to survive the journey.

The road is two lanes wide. There are four lanes of traffic using it. Our tuk-tuk driver overtakes and undertakes, regardless of the size and speed of other road users. At one stage, unable to pass a car in front by overtaking, the oncoming monster truck was even too big for him. He swerves the three-wheeled chariot along the inside of the car and onto the verge. There are no kerbs – tarmac finishes where dirt and rubbish begin. Our driver knows the road well. I hold on tight – watching his driving skill was mesmerising, manoeuvring his three-wheeled chariot with skill, excellence even.

On this manic stretch, there are strange combinations of goods on sale from roadside stalls. They are hawking carpets, rugs, and, strangely, giant soft toys – an interesting trio of wares. And not just an odd one or two. Too many for the quirky wares of a single shopkeeper.

Strung on ropes between the trees, mats are waving at us, while pink teddy bears – the size of a small adult, or a large child – relax back on plastic chairs underneath them. I could have reached out and grabbed a bear's hand. We were that close.

For a long time, we follow a bright yellow Piaggio Ape – the flatbed truck version of a tuk-tuk. A forlorn-looking man sits squashed up next to plastic buckets and a covering of tarpaulin. We are so close. From the rear seat, we lock eyes. He keeps eye contact a bit too long to feel comfortable as we pass.

There are no rules to roads in India bar one – you must pass the vehicle in front at all costs, even life I fear. Bonnets curved inwards from head-on collisions, the back ends missing completely from others. They validate my fear for our safety. We travel for twenty minutes along this road of death before turning off to the left.

The traffic slows. The driver edges forward as far as he can between a minibus carrying eight nuns, all looking like Mother Teresa, and a small saloon car with four generations of a family squashed inside. A level crossing barrier brought us to a standstill. Engine off and radio up. I soon understood why. The train took five minutes to arrive and another ten to pass. Then the barrier lifted. Lewis Hamilton would have been impressed with our start off the line. There was a tsunami surge forward by every kind of motorised and self-propelled transport you can imagine. The road opened up and soon we were driving alongside the canals famous in Alappuzha.

Beside the road stretches a familiar narrow green carpet – water hyacinth plants. Deep and thick, never guessing underneath was water. Attempting to hold back the advance of the curse of the backwaters is about as useless as trying to stop a river of lava flowing out of a volcano. The green monster wins every time.

The road undulates like a roller coaster. At each junction, where small bridges crossed the canal, the road would rise and fall – as did our stomachs. There are lots of bridges in Alappuzha! I count them. I'm just about holding everything in when we reach a major junction. Red traffic lights halt our journey. In the middle lane of three streams of traffic, all waiting and all eager, the driver motions with his left hand to get out. 'Here?' I say. The motion of his right hand reaching forward for my rupees gives me my answer.

The smell of diesel is overpowering. Metallic and distinctive, the fumes catch in the back of my throat and chokes the air as we rush out of the tuk-tuk. There is no simple or dignified way for this manoeuvre. Backwards seems the safest option. We step down into the middle of the road. Cars, motorbikes, and swarms of tuk-tuks surround us as the traffic lights change to green. Crowds swarm, jostling us as the chance to cross the busy road opens up. This is more like the India I imagined I might see. Most of the crowds are heading toward pavements full of street vendors. We follow them.

Walking a street in India is like twisting a kaleidoscope before your eye. From every roof billboards scream brands at you; mobile phone companies must have big advertising budgets here, their favoured colour red. Shop signs flashing neon messages swing precariously off the sides of buildings, each trying to catch your attention by outdoing the gaudiness of their neighbour's attempt.

There is a river of saris coming towards us, spanning the pallet of Picasso – deep ruby-reds, bubblegum pinks, other exquisite patterns, patchworks of golds and silvers. Bright oranges, ochres, and cobalt-blue stitches of gold thread glittering in the sun. The men dress in checked orange, red, and pink shirts, contrasting the snow-white dhotis tucked into waistbands.

In the air, the ever-present buzz of black and yellow tuk-tuks are flashing by like oversize bees. Great knots of spaghetti wire hang from telegraph poles surplus to requirement. The swaying loops look like oversized earrings. Here is my India, the India I wanted to see, to hear, and to smell. It's pungent, punctuated by smouldering incense and toxic diesel fumes, and I breathe it deep in, grateful to be here.

A spice seller spots us first. I suppose against the swell of colour around us, we stand out. There is a sign over our heads with an arrow pointing down, screaming tourist. In his hands is a star anise, imploring us forward to smell the dusty brown shape. He then presses pieces of cinnamon the size of lollipop sticks into our hands. I always thought it was a twig, not the bark of the tree dried and curling, giving it the shape. The distinctive aroma of Christmas candles and rice pudding surge up my nose. Huge barrels of spices fill the stall; there are more in the road than on the pavement. He points to small packets of spices hanging in dusty plastic bags on pegs. These look old, and I wonder if they have been there since Gandhi was nonviolently protesting against the British. I shake my head, and we carry on.

Standing back, admiring his work, a vegetable seller puts the finishing touches to his display. With all the finesse and precision of a watchmaker, he adds the ultimate piece of ginger to a sturdy pile two feet high.

Ginger grows as a root, each knuckle bulbous and misshapen, yet somehow he's balanced hundreds one on top of the other. The pride he is taking in his work displays in glorious colours and shapes. An artist. I wonder how many people bustling past notice the intricate work of his hands. Their colour and shape dictated the choice of vegetables stacking high next to each other. The contrast makes them more vibrant, the colours bolder, appealing, and mouth-wateringly desirable.

The stall is six vegetables wide and two vegetables deep. That doesn't account for the shiny aubergines held tightly by fistfuls of ladies' fingers grasping them from spreading over long spiky green bitter gourds, all pointing due North. At floor level, yellow lines on green marrows match each other straight as railway tracks. Suran, or elephant foot yams, one on top of the other, look like stacks of dried cow dung pancakes in towers. No way appetising by sight, yet if cooked, have the consistency of meat, so we were told. I'll give that possibility a miss.

He places every single vegetable with care, twists them with intention in the same way a master artisan working as a stonemason might chisel away at marble. Sweeping away piles of discarded outer leaves and damaged vegetables, now he stands back and admires it all – today's trading can begin.

It is a work of art, not a place of commerce. His is no ordinary vegetable display – it is a work of excellence. I believe that excellence matters. You find rosebuds where excellence thrives.

Falsely attributed to Aristotle (it was actually Will Durant) I often have quoted the words, 'We are what we repeatedly do. Excellence, then, is not an act, but a habit.' I've tried to work and live by that habit for many of the fifty-nine and three-quarters years of my life.

The pursuit of excellence – not perfection – is a two-edged sword. It can take you beyond being a healthy pursuit. Like winning the world hot dog eating championship. Joseph Christian Chestnut ate 71 hotdogs in 10 mins at Nathan's Hot Dog Eating Contest. Followed by six packets of anti-heartburn pills, four deposits in the bank account for a future heart attack, and a few hours in the toilet I would imagine. Winning first prize in a competition like that is a long-term loss.

Chasing perfection can be the same. The phrase, 'Oh, it will do...' or 'It's good enough,' is as annoying to me as waiting by a car parking space to come free and someone else whizzing in and stealing it – yes, that bad. Striving for excellence has its limits. But I still hold that excellence matters, though it's taken me fifty-nine and three quarters to tame it.

There is a point you reach when working has diminishing returns for the time invested. Say it takes 20 hours to get a project to 80% PSE (Pete's Scale of Excellence). To gain an extra 10% might take another 20 hours effort – it's not worth it. Settle at excellence. I know that now – I only wish I had learned it sooner. It's probable many work colleagues over the years wished I had as well. Too many times I pushed too many people, projects, and myself too far, not recognising the point of diminishing returns.

Excellence matters. Pushing for excellence is a worthy pursuit in life. Trying to strive for perfection is fruitless.

We feel it when someone takes an extra effort to focus on the details – it can be a rosebud moment. I once went to a business conference where they printed your name on both sides of the square laminated name badges dangling around necks. A simple idea. But attention to detail set the event organisers apart from most other conferences I've ever attended. (And I remembered.) Twisted or not, the name of the networking friend you had that uncomfortable conversation with was visible at all times. At least you didn't have to ask their name.

Excellence matters. Those little touches of excellence we don't always see, but when we experience them, when we feel them, they have an intrinsic quality, making projects and people stand out. Remarkable is rare.

Just like this vegetable seller in Alappuzha. There were other stalls in the road, but none looked like his. This was more than a job to him. He was an artist. He created his art here each day. It was his pursuit of excellence. He must have loved creating the display, day by day. Relentless unpacking, placing, twisting, and selling. If I had been in the market for buying, it would have made me stop and purchase. It was excellence in action. Not perfection, because a few tomatoes had wandered into the runner beans, and a cheeky pineapple was rubbing a bit too close to a cauliflower – but it was as close to perfection as you can get.

Excellence matters. Excellence is the border where rosebuds grow. We should say it when we see it, when we feel it. We should point those rosebuds out to others and gather them for ourselves. They're rare and precious.

Excellence matters.

Chapter 30

Are You Being Served?

The Aalin Thara Ganapathi, on Mullackal Road, is a Hindu temple to Krishna. It dwarfs all the surrounding buildings in size and also in beauty. I find it impossible not to stare at the structure and the devotees passing through the gates.

India has changed something soul level within me, never appreciating the artistic beauty of Hinduism before. I've seen faith expressed through the form of its architecture in many countries. I've stood in awe at the dome of the Sultan Ahmed Mosque – 'The Blue Mosque' – in Istanbul, at Buddhist temples in Vietnam, and Stupas in Katmandu. The Catholic Cathedrals of Florence and Santiago de Compostela take your breath away with the height of their vaulted ceilings and the vision the original architect had to build something so magnificent they would never see completed in their lifetimes. But as pilgrimage to sacred sites and temples is part of Hinduism and dharma, or way of life, these temples are different in how the external beauty of the buildings tells ancient stories through the statues covering them.

A gateway to the temple leads into a courtyard. Worshippers are flowing in and out, a constant stream of supplication and devotion. The temple's shape resembles an enormous cake, layer on layer, the colourful tiers climbing high. Around the edges at each level, the piercing stares of an army of statues are keeping watch. Lilacs, pastel pinks, deep turquoise greens, the statues hold artistic poses, some holding up the layer above them with arms outstretched. Archers on the backs of tigers stand next to women sitting in meditation.

There is a row of shops running alongside and underneath the temple. Above shop signs, the layers of statues continue on down the street. We stop opposite a pharmacy of sorts, the only shop with an English sign. Watching over the purchasing of pills and potions sits a gallery of the gods. Two roaring lions separate a line of deities. The crowds bustling, the traffic unending, we seem to be the only ones standing in awe at the spectacle of the temple.

I am next to a stall selling flower garlands for temple offerings. It spills out onto the road opposite the temple, bookended between spice sellers – the fragrance of marigolds fighting with the pungent overtones of curry leaf spice – for my attention. It is a flood of colour, a river of beauty against the slate-grey dust of the tarmac. The temple economy booms in India. Worshippers come daily to offer flowers to the gods. Tangerine and lemon marigold heads are overflowing large blue plastic buckets. Hanging from the arms of a tattered red and white parasol, finished garlands wait for a buyer, their new owners hoping to appease and please the gods. Behind the stall, threading and tying the flowers, and gaining a little shade from the heat under the canopy, an old man lifts a half-finished project, offering it towards me. A devotee, the sandalwood paste from the mornings offerings he made bright on his forehead, sticks of incense smouldering out and upwards from the floor offer a brief respite from the fumes he inhales each day.

Meandering the stores along the street, we walk into a few. Many we pass by, their trade not for us. Gold wedding jewellery to buy or hire is popular, and so it seems are pawn shops buying it back by the look of it. There are no other tourists around. The absence seems striking. We are the objects of attention again.

Spying shelves full of fabric bolts and cotton scarfs hanging from a display, we wander into a small shop. There is one narrow aisle between glass counters filled to capacity with wraps of material in order by colour. Piled high to the ceiling are saris wrapped in cellophane packets. Like books on a library shelf, you get a glimpse of a story from the cover, but only by opening would you get to see the genuine mysteries unfold.

Two young women behind the counter are laughing. The rhythm of their conversation pitching high and low, it sounds like they are almost singing the words. It is obvious they are having fun and turn their attention to us, smiling and bowing, hands in namaste position. They both wear beautiful saris with contrasting cotton scarfs draped around their necks and cascading down their backs. A simple design statement. We motion to the rainbow of scarfs hanging from displays, then pointing at theirs too.

Soon they are pulling multiple packets from the glass cases and spreading the samples out. Each scarf is a coil plait. The women unwrap the scarfs, shaking them like sheets in the air. Each is the same length and width, only the colours change – there is every shade and hue of colour imaginable. We pick five. I ask them to show us how to wear them. They mistake this for me asking how to coil them back up. They cast a glance at each other and, with one at each end, they twist the sheet of cotton as you would if you were wringing water out of it. As it twists, they laugh and giggle. It winds up with them meeting in the middle and one deftly folds with a few final curls, and it's back into a plait that you could fit into a handbag.

I point at the scarf around their necks, motioning to show me how to make it hang like theirs. The rupee drops. Now, understanding my request, they give us a fashion show – twenty ways to turn a scarf into a fashion accessory. I start to video them and they play to the camera, their laughter returning as each woman showed another style. It was like they were remembering how they experimented with fashion as teenagers. They suggest ideas to each other, helping pull the cotton around their shoulders and arms. They twist and turn like models on a catwalk with each new style. The purchase was a few pounds, the performance priceless.

Stretching across four floors, the department store selling silks and sarees was Nirvana for Noreen. Greeting us at the bottom of the entrance steps were porters in khaki military-style shirts. Distinguished by his combed white-grey hair and matching moustache the size of a small cat, a polite gentleman with two gold bars on his shoulders guides us into the throngs of busy shoppers.

Polished teak counters, an arm's length wide, line the walls on all sides. A sea of glass-topped counters fill the aisles between. Crowds bustle past. We see another collection of scarfs hanging from a display. Our porter, still with us, pulls the display down and spreads out the silk for Noreen to see and feel. She picks another five – we had been in the store for three minutes and twenty seconds.

The porter took the scarfs, beckoning us to follow him, and leads us towards a long sales counter with a polished mahogany surface. He hands over our scarfs and, faster than we can see it happen, they return wrapped in brown paper, Sellotape sealing the neat square package tight. Along with the parcel, we have an A4 invoice printed on a dot matrix printer. We take two steps to the left. He hands the invoice and our parcel back across the counter with our few rupees. There is a process of bureaucracy that cannot be shortcut here; I can feel it. Our parcel returns wrapped in a brown paper bag. The temptation of another three floors of this cotton emporium was too tempting to resist. We walk towards a substantial staircase.

First Floor – Wedding Sarees. The noise, excitement, and atmosphere of joy greeting you off the stairs soon betrayed the sign. A gaggle of young women are poring over various shades of plum-purple sarees spread wide over the counter. Animated and loud, they giggle and squeal, holding the material against them, twirling coy looks at each other, the silver embroidery and the gold embellishments reflecting in mirrors on columns. Each saree is a tapestry of creativity, an individual work of art. Roadside billboards two storeys high sell wedding day dreams. Shopping here is the fulfilment of that dream sold in the skies.

Behind the group of young women sit uninterested, visibly bored young men staring into mobile phones. The same scene is repeated in every department store in the world – here though is a square of comfortable sofas for them. They are here for the day.

Across the aisle, an assistant is spreading a fuchsia pink and gold saree out for Noreen. There are yards of the material in one long river of colour. We were going to buy it the instant he got it out of the packet.

Second Floor – Cotton Fabric. We have more odd pieces of fabric in our loft than the cutting room of the wardrobe department for Strictly Come Dancing. Crafts and Noreen go together like cheese and onion, gin and tonic, a 14-year-old boy and Clearasil. The opportunity of endless squares of fabric coming her way is sparking neurological carnivals to go off in her brain. Like Michelangelo looking at a block of marble and seeing David, Noreen can look into a bag of fabric and see tote bags, makeup pouches with zippers, and the most exquisite hearts of every size. More wrapped brown paper packages appear and disappear.

Top Floor – More Cotton Fabric. The top floor was quieter. The bolts of cloth for sale stood vertically on shelves that lined the walls. It was a Library of Congress of colours. A box on the end of the counter contained Fat Quarters, individually wrapped in cellophane packets. At around seventeen pence each – a steal. I would have bet the farm, though I don't own one, on the certainty we would leave with a collection. We did. The service was pure Indian – kind, peaceful, and done with a smile.

Fabric shopping complete, our next quest was to find the only other item on our shopping list – umbrellas.

Little did we know the treasure trove we were about to uncover when we entered the world of the Umbrella Kings of Kerala.

Chapter 31

Let the Rains Come

Like video streaming on a mobile phone with a poor signal, the heat of the day sucked all remaining energy from us. Tired and weighted down with fabric wrapped in brown paper parcels, I was exhausted. We should have been more adventurous than a burger for lunch. I think our stomachs could have managed some local delicacies. It seemed the best option, looking around. There was the faint idea of meat, but with an aroma more of old tea bags than beef. Not a glimmer of a rosebud in sight.

I had given up hope. The possibility of finding the umbrellas Noreen had in mind was fading fast amid the toxic fumes, itching dust, and unrelenting stares. We were passing many women carrying these works of art, these moving canopies of visual delight. Filigree lines, gold and silver, sunshades you could hang up for their innate beauty. Our mission was to find the same. Right now, I wouldn't have cared if I could have sat under the shade of one with a silhouette of Mother Rapper on. But our quest was one I was ready to give up on.

Reaching the end of Mullackal Road, needing to decide left or right, we nod to the only other tourists we see all day – well, tourists that stand out as much as being tourists as we do. I'm guessing they were a Scandinavian family, Norwegian flags on their backpacks, all three blond-haired, powerful features, good boots. I'm guessing they were lost – the gigantic map the father was carrying was a bit of giveaway. It surprised them as much to spot other tourists. The absence of tourists was starting to become a worry, the exodus all too evident. The 'virus' now had a name and a number - COVID-19, and it was scaring everyone away. Adding to the natural worry and unrest for local people around us was the pressure of tourist rupees disappearing just as fast. We could feel the fear, the uncertainty rising. What I didn't like was the growing waves of panic starting to roll in along with it.

I'm ready to flag down the first tuk-tuk driver passing us. It is a joint decision to give up the umbrella quest. I look in both directions; not a vehicle in sight. This is a mystery. Any other moment swarms buzz by, seeking the next fare. Not a three-wheeled taxi in sight. As often happens, serendipity favours the curious. So, noticing a few more shops further to the right, I suggest we should carry on walking in the direction it feels like we should head, no rhyme or reason, just homing pigeon instincts.

Shops in India spill out onto pavements and into roads. Standing out against the surrounding chaos, gleaming stainless-steel rails sweep up a rather grand-looking staircase away from the pavement and up towards a sizeable glass-fronted shop, and in the window a display of umbrellas. Not quite the kind Noreen had in mind, however. These were smaller versions of ceremonial umbrellas that tower above elephant howdahs at festivals. But promising, our optimism rising as the door handle we twist is in the shape of an umbrella.

Scraping across a thick mat, it felt we were entering a luxury car showroom – hurricane cold blasts of air conditioning and polished marble floors. Not a car in sight. The only item for sale was umbrellas. We'd stumbled across a shrine to the brolly, a temple to the sun shade. By sheer chance and the luck of the parasol gods shining on us, we were standing in the head office and main shop of none other than one of the Umbrella Kings of Kerala – John's Umbrella Mart.

A large photograph hangs prominently opposite us. The unblinking eyes of a dignified-looking gentleman, his Nehru jacket fading grey rather than the white when the portrait taken, watches over three women sales assistants ready and eager to serve us. Is this John, I wonder? The story of the umbrella kings of Kerala is a one of family rivalry, intense competition, and creative marketing driving innovation around a single product – the humble umbrella. It begins back in the days of the British rule. It now thrives through two cousins and two businesses – Popy's Umbrella Mart and John's Umbrella Mart.

The Kerala monsoons arrive each year. It rains for weeks, the prefect climate you would consider for starting an umbrella business. Kasim Karim Settu and Thayyil Abraham Varghese were running an umbrella business in Alappuzha, Kerala, in the days when the British ruled India. To manufacture an umbrella of the highest quality was their pursuit of excellence. When the Raj was over and independence was splitting the country and families apart, Kasim Karim Settu left for the newly formed Pakistan. He sold his share of the business to Abraham Verghese and a textile business owner, Kumara Swamy Reddiar. So began the 'Radhakrishna Umbrella Mart.'

Whether it was in admiration of the days of British rule in India, I'm not sure. But when Abraham left to start his own venture in 1954, he called it the 'St George Umbrella Mart.' Abraham's umbrellas were renowned for their quality. Soon his two sons joined him. The quality, design, and style of their umbrellas was unmatched in Kerala and much of India.

It was Abraham who was watching over us from his portrait. When he passed away, the business spilt between his two sons – Baby and Abraham, who would go their separate ways, Baby setting up Popy's Umbrella Mart and Abraham setting up John's Umbrella Mart. Today the grandsons of Abraham Verghese lead these businesses. While there is fierce rivalry and competition, innovation for customer satisfaction is the goal, not just profits.

You would think umbrella design focuses only on the canopy colours and designs. To a large extent it is. But both manufacturers scored big when they landed the sole Indian rights to Walt Disney, Marvel, DC, and Star Wars to reproduce children's favourite characters on the umbrellas. But their creativity didn't stop there. Popy's invented an 'Uncle' – a children's customer representative. Kids could phone him and he would have a conversation with them about their favourite brolly. Rivalry spurned on innovation. One umbrella mart would make umbrellas that sprayed water or emitted lights. The other would release a brolly playing music with an MP3 player and speaker built in. Another even popped out table-tennis sized balls, all at the press of a button! The '007 Special' had a handle the shape of the stock of a rifle barrel. They even added GPS or selfie sticks on others. Capitalising on the rise of the mobile phone and internet, they both made advertising jingles that went viral online. Now the competition is driving innovation to make the smallest and lightest full-size umbrellas. It was these that would save the day and bring our quest to a successful completion.

It feels overpowering, as three sales assistants to one customer are opening sample after sample to show Noreen. Lined up along the counter popping them open, my eyes blur; the splashes of colours are paining me the way you get prism shards of light at the periphery of sight sometimes.

'Do you have any with elephants on?' Noreen asks. Everything but. Hanging by smooth wooden handles behind the counter squeezed side by side pencils of colour – polka dots, tartans, floral, and plain. I'm wondering by the second how we are ever going to get three of these magnificent accessories home. In the corner was a display of collapsible umbrellas. We narrowed it down to four – and yes, there were elephants.

The final decision was tough. We agreed on three. Entering the purchases into a computer, they handed us an A4 invoice printed out on a dot matrix printer. Déjà vu moment approaching. A henna-painted hand is motioning we should pass this invoice along the counter to a serious-looking man staring into a computer screen. At a stretch, he must have been three feet from where the sale took place. The shop wasn't bursting with customers; we were the only ones, the rainy season a month or more away. We alone were shoppers. He must have seen us. But there was the look of utter surprise on his face, as much as questioning us 'You've brought umbrellas?' I'm not sure if he and wife were arguing before work, or the tuk-tuk was late arriving, but if he had been one of the seven dwarfs he certainly wouldn't have been Happy. He was the keeper of the key to the draw where they kept the money, and that was a man's job here.

We paid him. Fabric and umbrellas, our quest was now finally complete. Time to go home.

It's our last night at the homestay. Tomorrow we head for Cochin and begin the journey home. The smell of incense is drifting from under the table across to where the pool lights are reflecting on the surface of the water. It was a beautiful evening to sip a cold Kingfisher beer. In the distance, a gentle flute was playing a call to prayer. Suddenly, at earsplitting decibels over a P.A. we hear, 'Jesus wants me for a sunbeam,' or something like that in Malayalam.

And if the Mother of all Rappers starts tonight, Jesus is going to gain one soon.

Chapter 32

The Phone Call

Now I'm ready to return home, and that's a comforting feeling.

Packing our bags after breakfast, clothes we had carried across the world and never used, scrunched and creased, are hidden by umbrellas and fabric. We said our goodbyes to Allwyn and Jency. Posing for photographs by the pool, the three days to rest and relax to 'fly and flop' we had spent with them had been perfect. The food, accommodation, and experiences added together. It was like taking adding two and two and making six – far better than any expectations I'd had before we arrived.

There was a change in the air. We all felt it. An unspoken sadness between friends, both knowing something was not right, but not wanting to name it, to make it appear by talking about it. We just said goodbye. The virus spreading across the world was here, it was in Kerala, and we were leaving. But what about those who would stay? For those who call this home, the feeling not of comfort, but safety and security the topic of conversations. The fear of tourist rupees fleeing was replaced by fear alone.

We had one day left, and I want to experience India to the last moment. Allwyn had arranged for the taxi to take us to visit the old port area, Bazaar Street and Jew Town at Fort Kochi an hour and a half away. The driver was going to stay with us all day. He would keep our cases in his car, pick us up in the afternoon and then drop us off at the airport hotel – we had an early flight the following day. At around £50 for the travel and time, it was excellent value. As I was to learn, it was more helpful than I could have imagined as we first climbed into the small white taxi.

The atmosphere in the taxi was thick; it felt like someone was trying to spoon cold golden syrup out of a tin. Sticky, unmoving, and unrelenting, not giving up anything for the effort. No gods on the dashboard to offer prayers and supplication. No conversation with nervous British passengers in the rear. The language barrier was doing nothing to disguise the agitation in the driver's voice. There was a problem – and the person on the other end of the mobile phone call was not offering any help with the problem, not giving anything for the effort of the conversation.

It was disconcerting sitting together in the rear of a taxi travelling the main road that heads North-South along the coast at rush hour. If there is a rush hour – it seems chaotic any time of the day – but certainly the time for commuting. Whenever I will think back on India, two things will always be forefront – colours and traffic. I would have added smiles, but after Allwyn telling me smiles were only covering sadness, I was not so sure now about receiving smiles from everyone we met and now waved to us from the roadside.

Our first stop took us further away from Fort Kochi, our destination for the day, back to Alappuzha, and back to John's Umbrella Mart. We should have purchased the fourth umbrella. It's hard to shop quickly at John's, the same purchasing routine repeating, the same look of utter surprise we have purchased umbrellas from the cashier. Soon we were heading in the right direction, if not starting back twenty minutes in the wrong direction. But we had another John's umbrella.

The driver's mobile phone tone trilled like a bird, whistling, cawing, and calling for his attention. The first phone call, I later found out, was from his wife. She was calling to say he needed to phone the bank – and quick. It was the first bank call that did not go well. Not only the first call, but the many he would have over the hour and a half we were sitting in the back of the taxi. On each call, the tension and intensity of the conversation rose before halting as the driver or the person at the other end cut the call.

On another day, and under different circumstances, I would have asked to stop so we could look at the places we were passing. Long bridges gave a view of the sea on one side, the backwaters on the other. We passed an elaborate and imposing temple in full preparations for a festival, streams of bunting hanging from the entrance gates at which six elephant transport trucks were lined up. The trucks high off the road, flatbed and bright yellow, had signs written along the side in red – Elephant Transport. I think they would have been redundant had one passed you along the busy roads, its cargo standing in the open back. Looking at the map on my phone and the distance to the hotel it would make the trip back later difficult but not impossible. The opportunity of seeing six 'tuskers' at a festival was tempting.

The phone went again – it broke into my thoughts and stole the moment like a thief at night.

The driver was wearing a Bluetooth headset. He might have had two hands on the steering wheel, but his mind was somewhere else. He raised again the volume of his voice. It's difficult to guess the content of a conversation by the sound of voices speaking in another language. The nuances of the culture can make some conversations sound like fierce arguments when they are nothing of the kind. But adding together facial expressions, body language, and tone and you can get a picture. The picture that I got was our driver was moving away from anger to something that was more pleading, desperate, and heading towards begging. Lost in his conversation, forgetting we were sitting in the back, party to the words, catching my eye in his rear-view mirror and cutting the call one more time, he turned his head and told us what was happening. He could speak excellent English. People were leaving Kerala and India in a panic, he told us, his face filled with fear.

The first reports of the virus in India were from Kerala. Back in January, they tested two students returning from Wuhan in China and found them positive. Like much of the world then, the virus was something happening out there, but it was not then the global pandemic threat it would become.

We could not rely on the news we were reading in glimpsed headlines. We had read a list of the countries where the virus was worst. According to one Indian newspaper, the Diamond Princess Cruise liner was the third biggest country infected by the virus. (I'm not sure the journalist understood it was a cruise liner stuck offshore.) Panic was setting in and we were somewhat oblivious. It started as we were arriving in India. But not reading the web, or newspapers, we were unaware of the extent of the exodus of tourists taking place.

Our driver was. Within three weeks, his trade had all but disappeared. Along with it went any capacity to earn money. Living only by what he could earn day by each day, there was no buffer between him, his family, and ruin. The bank was demanding the monthly payment for his car loan. He hadn't got enough money to buy food for his family for today. He was trying to delay the payment, but the bank was not offering any help. Deep furrows etched in his frown and there was a darkness in his eyes as he glanced backwards. If they took his car, he would lose all possibility of earning any income – and they were threatening to do so.

As the driver was navigating the final busy streets of our journey, the phone went again. His voice was soon lost in the throes of another conversation. He stopped on a sharp bend, motioning for us to get out. We saw him driving away, animated in conversation, and though we didn't say it, we both were wondering if we would see him and our cases later as we had arranged.

Chapter 33

God's Chosen Few

SPICES LIKE PEPPER AND cinnamon would entice traders, merchants, and opportunists to sail the dangerous voyage from Europe to India in search of these aromatic treasures. For those successful in reaching their destination, great wealth could follow. For many, it would be their last journey.

In 1498 Vasco da Gama, the Portuguese explorer, established the first sea route to Kerala – their destination Fort Kochi. The Portuguese began a monopoly on the world spice trade for decades; it marked the beginning of a colonial era of Kerala, taking almost 450 years for it to end.

Today a richness of ethnic diversity lives in Kochi – fifteen different ethnic communities call Kochi their home, tracing ancestors back to Romans, Egyptians, Chinese, and Persians among others. The Chinese came and left their fishing nets. The Dutch came and left Mattancherry Palace. You see these foreign influences sauntering around Fort Kochi in the buildings, the culture, and religion. As one former mayor calls it, Fort Kochi is 'a cultural mosaic.' The mixing of religious tiles of Hinduism, Judaism, Islam, and Christianity create an open tolerance of space for each other, the temples, churches, synagogues, and mosques sitting beside each other as much in peace it feels as the people.

But before Europeans, the Jews had already arrived. Israelites were trading between King Solomon's kingdom and India as far back as 952 BCE. The Jews in Kochi are the oldest community of Jews in India. Persecution of the Jewish nation is as old as time. In 1492, after the expulsion of many Jews from Europe, Jewish traders and families followed new trade routes, and a community found their way to Kochi. These are the 'Paradesi Jews,' or foreign Jews. They built successful businesses, palatial homes, and impressive synagogues in Jew Town in Fort Kochi.

Where our driver stopped was at the entrance to the Jewish community, a district full of bazaars, street art, and cosy coffee shops, so the guidebooks say. Watch out for crowds and pick-pockets, it added. The buzz of trade and people sounded like the best last day for our India adventure. It never even reached a hum.

On the corner of Synagogue Lane and Jew Town Road, fading almost to invisibility, a sign pointed us towards 'Jew Street.' Underneath it, much larger and bolder, a proclamation told us we were walking towards 'God's Own Country.' I think we are in the right district. The signs could have read Ghost Town or Mary Celeste Row for the all the people in sight. Deserted. It felt as downcast as the faces on shopkeepers sitting on kerbs watching us. No worries about pickpockets here today.

Jew Street is straight, narrow, and a few strides wide. The short street ends at Paradesi Synagogue. Either side are a few tacky tourist shops selling the things you wonder who buys. No cars or tuk-tuks, only pedestrians. We are the only two. As faded as the signpost, it gave off an aura of being run-down rather than historic, the roofs and buildings hanging over the pavement like the hooked eyebrows of an old man who has seen too many years and feels as desperate for life as the shopkeepers were below.

Appearing outside each shop were optimistic, expectant traders. Those not staring into mobile phones were staring at us. We walked the gauntlet. 'Come look, no need to buy' suggested signs above doors – 'hassle-free shopping' offered others. The signs were in English, Hebrew, and Malayalam. I awarded 'Best Sign of The Day' to the souvenir shop owner who wrote 'No Blah Blah Blah' above his door. We wave off the invites, though to be truthful they were halfhearted, fruitless requests. We throw a few crumbs of hope offering to look when we come back. That's always a mistake – say 'No.'

Slightly intimidated by being the centre and focus of attention, we are relieved to find the entrance to the cafe and skip up the dark staircase to the first floor.

Reading about a famous art coffee shop while planning, its calling cards the vibe of the place and being a local hangout for artists displaying their work, it seemed the perfect place to soak in the atmosphere, an interesting stop to observe life over a drink. It was empty. Empty of people and any semblance of atmosphere. A vacuum of personality in people and place.

Staring into his mobile phone slouched across the counter, the only other breathing, sentient being seemed irritated someone wanted coffee. It had potential. Long empty tables lined the side wall where above them hundreds of individual plants, hanging like a waterfall of green, cascaded down. If they were real, and I think they were, at least something else was alive in here. Industrial lighting, hanging slightly above head height, made it feel more like a coffee shop in Camden market, London than a Jewish Bazaar district in Kerala, India.

Photos of 'celebrities' – none I recognised – were looking down eating enormous, sumptuous meals. But not today. The coffee was excellent, but the atmosphere felt anything but. There was a wandering sadness about the place, a heavyweight feeling of loss that was pervading everything, sticking to the walls, ceilings, and floors. Even the clanking of pots and pans in the kitchen by an invisible chef was halfhearted that morning. The struggling cloak of sadness remained with us for the remaining hours in Fort Kochi – and to be truthful – in India.

The persecution of Jews since the dawning of time, according to Scripture, is a mystery to me. My head understands it, but my heart rejects it. The awareness of injustice and persecution began with felt cutouts placed on a green baize board at Sunday School. The Jews, I was told, are 'God's Chosen People.' It was during my studies, however, it gained a new seriousness when researching the history of the Jewish nation became material central for my theology degree at Birmingham University.

Those three years were a steep learning curve in academic skills, but I relished the ascent each day. It was an Everest of a climb involving a semester in my second year studying the roots of the holocaust during World War II. Those few weeks changed me forever. While I now understand 'how' the propaganda, systematic racism, and lying rhetoric inflamed a fire of hatred so evil it didn't burn out until six million or more Jews and innocents died, I'll never understand 'why' the persecution of one nation of people would continue for centuries.

I have been fortunate to visit Israel on two occasions. Once, I also went to Auschwitz concentration camp in Poland. People ask me, why would you want to visit a concentration camp? 'Because we must never forget the Holocaust,' is my reply. We must never forget. By visiting, telling, and retelling the stories of each individual the history and their history remains. And it should, it must. To stand as a warning to future generations.

So, I know it will sound strange, but after leaving the coffee shop the next place I wanted to visit was a cemetery. The sign pointing to a Jewish Cemetery in Fort Kochi caught my eye. I had to go. I had to visit there before we did any shopping or more sightseeing.

Unsurprising, The Gan Shalom Jewish Cemetery is on Jew Street. Gan Shalom, as best as I can understand, describes a garden of peace. The high black ornate gates were closed. The cemetery, peering through the bars, needed care and was overgrown in places. 'Sorry visitors are not allowed,' said a large yellow sign turning me away. On concrete pillars either side, they carved an inscription. On one side in Hebrew, on the other, English.

'The compound wall and shed inside erected by Jacob Hai Ephraim Cohen to the memory of his father – Mr Ephraim Daniel Cohen and his sister Miriam – May their souls rest in peace. 15 September 1896.'

Ephraim Daniel Cohen was a leading Jewish merchant in Cochin. The last person buried in the cemetery was also a Cohen – Sarah Cohen. Sarah was the last Paradesi Jew living in Fort Kochi, the last of generations of Jews that arrived before the Portuguese. It was not her death that made her known in Fort Kochi, but her life. She was an embroiderer.

We passed 'Sarah's Hand Embroidery' shop walking towards the cafe. It was difficult to miss. The bright blue sign advertising Jewish special items, Hallah Covers, Kippas, and tablecloths that had a Star of David at the top and a large painting of a menorah at the bottom. Though it described its wares, I preferred the shop's previous name. An old black and white photograph stuck to a wooden board outside the shop told me once they called it 'Sarah's Embroidery Fancy Centre.'

Sarah Cohen died on August 30 2019 – she was 96. At least four generations going back over 200 years of her family lived in Jew Town in the district of Mattancherry before her. They buried Sarah in the corner of the Gan Shalom Jewish Cemetery next to her husband. The consul general of Israel in Mumbai at the time placed a fistful of earth from Israel over her coffin. The end of a life, but more of an era.

Jew town now, allegedly, has two Paradesi Jews remaining, who live away from the area most of the year. The disappearance of the Paradesi Jews in Kochi started with the founding of Israel. God's chosen few in 'God's Own Country' – an Indian promised land.

And now Sarah has gone too.

Chapter 34

Bazaar, Bollywood, Or Bust?

A scrum of teenage boys jostle past us. One, with an expensive-looking camera, is pointing it at another framed in the doorway of a derelict spice warehouse. The rest are shouting directions on the way he should stand. They mimic how to put his arms above his head or move his legs. Long black hair waterfalls over his face. The young man doesn't have the bulk of a someone who lifts weights, but he is lean, tall, and his bottomless eyes have serious heat to melt hearts. He seems to know it too. He has a presence about him – even for someone around 16 or 17 years old at a guess. Wandering around the lanes on that hot afternoon, he was as sultry as the day. We see the group posing at different locations. An Instagram feed will no doubt sharing the images across the world.

We head back to Synagogue Lane. Though not alone now, the traffic flow of tourists is as meagre as the trade. The collection of shops sell the same bright coloured pashminas and baggy trousers, displaying them optimistically on manikins and in window displays. White linen smock shirts hanging high on hooks are like ghosts waving, trying to catch our attention. Desperate for a sale, the traders and shopkeepers stand outside, still offering no hassle shopping, but their calls to 'Come and look,' and 'You promised you would come in when you came back,' echoed in the emptiness.

I study a window display of dusty wooden artefacts and handicrafts, intricate carvings of rosewood and buffalo horn of gods lined up for sale. Standing next to Ganesh and Lord Shiva is Jesus, Mary and a monk, all vying for space and attention. Though if you were looking for a god by price, in this shop a monk is your best option.

Next door, little pyramids of vivid coloured powder – fluorescent fuchsia, a deep purple, cool teal, and fiery orange – are ablaze outside Imran Perfumes. Boxes of handmade natural incense sticks and essential oils fill the air with a heady mystical aroma as we pass, the spell broken by the shopkeeper imploring us to go inside to watch her make incense sticks. We know it would not be enough to watch her. Feeling for her humanity and to avoid the awkwardness of not wanting to buy after no doubt her skilful demonstration – handmade or not – we decline the offer. We were not in the market for incense sticks, but something else from the opposite side of the street caught my eye.

A gallery of portrait photographs clustered together in groups called for my attention. These were no ordinary snaps. Not studio shots either, but an intimate study of a people with a history. Deep lines on the faces of old men and women wrote long narratives of sadness, loss, despair, and pain. Children's faces seemed unable to smile. It's the one remaining emotion children continue to hold when their parents have long lost theirs. In the backgrounds, dilapidated stone shacks, wood fires smoking outside, clung precariously to mountainsides as skinny goats grazed on dust. Large format photographs, 8x10 at least. These were art, not photographs. They were not even for sale. I studied them for a long time, unaware of a young man perched on a large embroidered cushion outside the shop.

'My brother took these,' he said, adding, 'It was our way out of Afghanistan. He works for National Geographic as a photographer now. I have this shop. Come and see some clothes that come from my home village.'

Entering the small narrow space bright tapestries were hung on the walls, like a collection of flags from a nation called Hope. Intricate embroidered jackets and shawls swayed as we walked past, impossible to not rub against in the space. Weighty woollen blankets contrasted against sheer silk blouses. Every item was vying for your attention. Urgent and tightly packed, there was no space unfilled. It made you cautious of moving anything for fear of the entire stock to fall to your feet.

At floor level, covered poufs of soft leather and sequin embroidered cushion squares were snuggling up against crystallised rock formations the size of an enormous cat. Baskets overflowing with polished stones, blue lapis lazuli, and emeralds filled every space in between. Picking up one large smooth stone, he handed it to me. 'This is from my village,' he said. 'It's not precious in value, but it makes me think of home, where I came from. That is why I sell them.'

His English was simple, short sentences, the way a child might speak, but with a strong accent and almost in a whisper. I never asked his name. His name was important. I regret now I didn't ask him. I wonder the challenging route he took to arrive here? The thought was not lost on me he was now living in a community of people where for centuries it has been a place of tolerance and safety. His transitory story was unique to him but replicated uncountable times for others with not such a happy ending. Was this a happy ending?

He and his brother had fled Afghanistan as refugees, leaving the war and carnage raging behind them. Did he leave his family behind? Were they the gallery of faces? He didn't say, and I'm sorry I didn't ask. Was the story even real? It felt so. The photographs were not stock footage, more an essay of life, a passport that got them from a war zone to India. I wish I had more to tell of that story.

We chatted a little longer about the items he had for sale, how they were providing income for people from his village. We were not buyers. I didn't realise then how much I was in the market for one of those polished stones. I'm sad there isn't one sitting on the desk next to me as I write these words.

Crossing the narrow street, gazing at a few more statues huddling together in artefact bazaars, we enter a cavernous shop that would not have looked out of place in a top-end shopping centre in somewhere like Chelsea, Bath, or Cheltenham Spa. It was a clothing store. Made locally, each item was organic cotton. The tasteful window display had block printed shirts, scarfs, and dresses draped over sofas. Through them we could see many more hanging loosely on hooks, easy to flick through. Eager, itchy, almost too pleased to welcome us as we walked in, a young man dressed in a shirt like those on display asked if we wanted to see the process for printing the cottons. 'You've just come from my brother's shop,' he said. There was another story there. Was his 'brother' his brother? Or a term of endearment?

They had covered large workstations the size of table tennis tables in white linen, then were stamping them with deep blue geometric designs. I had a feeling this was more for show than production. On a rack of men's clothes, I caught sight of a magnificent cotton shirt. In that split second, they made the sale. I knew it – so did the assistant, though I had picked up nothing nor tried anything on. Another older guy, watching my eyes I guess, came in for the kill. I would not have freed a group of hostages with my negotiating skills, a halfhearted barter, but I knew there was some room in the price he offered me. 'You are the first sale of the day,' said the older guy. It was well past lunchtime. 'You are the only people to have been in shop.' On that basis, his sales ratio was impressive – 1 for 1. Looking up and down Jew Town Road as we left, bag in hand, I was not optimistic for any more sales that day. Few people were walking around, most of them locals and not tourists.

Jew Town Road snakes away from Synagogue Lane and runs parallel to the waterway between Fort Kochi and Willingdon Island. Its claim to fame is being the largest artificial island in India and a shipping port. We keep catching sight of the tankers and cranes through gaps in between dilapidated buildings sauntering towards a late lunch at Hotel Seagull. It is where we are expecting to meet our cases, hopefully, along with the driver to take us to our eventual stop, an airport hotel.

A few market stalls clump together alongside the road, each filled with serious tourist tack and plastic toys. They spill out away from the road and along a long jetty where tour boats rise and fall as container tankers pass. Wanting to get a better view of the city, we dodge the hawkers with little resistance. At the water's edge, a few men are sleeping curled up on concrete benches in what little shade there is. It is not the slumber of a siesta; I think they have given up on the possibility of any passengers.

The 'comfort station' in Munnar town looked like toilets of the rich and famous compared to the building housing the 'comfort station' on Mattancherry Boat Jetty. For 'GENS & LADIES' said the invitation along with 'Pay & Use' on the sign pointing across a patch of scrubland. A gauntlet of feral dogs were standing on parade, waiting to give a salute of kinds when you dared pass. I'm now thinking the rabies injections could have been a sound investment had I needed any 'comfort' that day. I decide the choice of wetting my pants seems a better option.

My children tease me about the phrase, 'Look at the architecture!' They echo my words, not my excitement, when I'm discovering any interesting building down some alley or back street on our travels. There is such beauty in doors – old doors opened and closed on many years, and lives. I have many times bumped into things on the ground – lampposts, people – looking upwards at buildings and moving forward at the same time.

When Jew Town Road emptied of the tacky market stalls and became Bazaar Road, full of run-down warehouses, dark alleys, mysterious passages, and broken doors, I was in my element. This is the commercial district of Fort Kochi – old, unchanged, and certainly not on the tourist trail, though you couldn't tell we were the only ones venturing.

Buzzing close past us on mopeds the photoshoot boys arrive. They stop outside a broken building, bowing towards the ground, the roof caved in from the weight of the forest of weeds overtaking and growing on top. Soon their future Bollywood star friend poses to command and direction. Peeping around shattered beams, backward glances across disjointed walls – a new location for the Instagram feed.

We pass the shell of a once impressive synagogue. Now only four walls remain, but on the gable end a Star of David still visible proclaims the history of the building and its people. Boarded-up buildings once painted daffodil yellow, odd blue shutters still at the windows, are whispering how vibrant the district must have looked in previous days. Now creeping green mildew and mould climbs the walls, devouring the colours.

Short corrugated roofs rust above door entrances where faded business signs hang. V Dasa Prabhu & Sons Tea Merchants – Estd 1721, Chettiar & Co sugar merchants, with A.R. Chockalingam Chettiar Sons – Estd 1906 in smaller text underneath. Behind the closed eyes of shuttered windows other wholesale businesses were still open for trade. Outside one building, two porters were asleep in a giant wheelbarrow big enough for them to doze side by side, sacks of rice, tea, and tobacco left in the heat of the sun waiting for the afternoon nap to finish. A family of goats find a place to sleep on top of the sacks. Inside the darkness of the rooms, I see stacked high more dusty hessian sacks. By the aroma wafting towards me from the doorway, they were full of spices.

We cross the small bridge over Calvatty Canal, the entry point for many spice traders from across the world. The heat of the day is now oppressive, the walk longer than I imagined. Even with the true fascination of the area, relieved, we turn the corner and find the famous Hotel Seagull, our ultimate destination.

The Hotel Seagull is over 200 years old. The dining area is on a pier that has views across the waterfront towards Cochi. That is itself a good enough reason to eat there – the other, more important reason is that it is one of only a couple licensed restaurants around. From the table behind us, a group of young guys were loud. They had finished a few already. They were playing a game called 'let's see how many empty Kingfisher beer bottles we can line up on the table.' We joined them – not at the table or in the game – but certainly with a Kingfisher beer. By the time we had eaten lunch and were ready for the taxi to arrive, it was The Hotel Seagull that had won – the profit on the beers making up for the general poor trade of the day. All we need now are our cases and our driver.

Chapter 35

The Long Road Home

Roads leading into airports really are the same the world over. Billboards, freight company offices and generic airport hotels. The empty office windows, deserted petrol stations, and overflowing car rental car parks flash by slowly, the scenes disconcerting. It replaced the air of excited anticipation leaving the airport terminal with something incomparable heading back. Despair. Dread. The silence outside and inside the car is deafening.

The journey from Fort Kochi took about an hour. No phone calls. No conversation. I wanted to ask about the bank. His eyes never glanced backwards. His shoulders slouched, hanging as if they tied two weights to them, now driving on automatic pilot. A resigned despondency held heavy in the air. I decided the silence said it all.

Dropping us off under the portico of the hotel, we tip him with generosity. No questions or complaints about old notes. His face lifted for a second; bringing his hands together, he whispers, 'Namaste.' We said goodbye. His worry was transferring on to us. I want to go home. I'm ready for home. It's a long journey, and it can't come soon enough.

It's that moment when thoughts of home come to mind. Within a rumbling rumination sits a blessing and gratitude to have travelled – but more, more you have a home to travel towards. You just want to be in your home, your bed, but without the travel.

We wanted to be at home. We wanted to feel safe. The overriding uncertainty now named and numbered. 'The Virus' had got to us as well. We had a phone call from someone concerned about our welfare. 'Do you know what's happening in the world? It's not a dose of the flu. You need to be vigilant,' he said. That worried us even more.

Roads leading in and out of airports are similar, but not all airport hotels are. Arriving late or departing early, an airport hotel is a functional stay. You want to sleep. You don't want to stay for two weeks. Turning to follow our cases into what resembles the lobby of a hotel, we enter, instead, a concept furniture store, empty of personality and devoid of people.

The cavernous reception stretches up into an open space, four or five floors high, and feels the width of a football field. Stylish for certain, practical I'm not so sure. The hotel might have won first place in a 'How to use furniture and fittings that look stylish but have no practical value' competition. My footsteps echo on the marble floors. Strange, because the soles of my shoes were soft rubber. A squeak maybe, but an echo?

A waterfall fills one wall. The source of this Niagara feature is on the second floor. It wasn't working. The size of drop and amount of water needed to cascade down, I can imagine why. The rush of water would have drowned out all possibility of hearing any conversation in this silent space. In the distance, almost out of sight, two cases wait at a reception desk.

A polished mahogany counter is the height of my shoulders. Reaching up, I hand over the passports. It felt like a small child reaching on to a kitchen counter trying to grab a biscuit. We were back in the world of branded polo shirts. Taking the scene in around me, I could only imagine the named wares on offer in the bathroom where we would head – hopefully soon. Tired and hot, we were ready to rest.

A voice coming somewhere from behind the counter offered soothing words – 'We've upgraded your room.' Peeping over the counter, looking down on us, he added, 'Have a seat over there. The porter will take your cases to the room.'

The row of tub-style chairs had a rake on the seat cushion at a steep angle facing downwards. Adverts for powered chairs to lift and tilt, helping the old or infirm stand up, came to mind. These chairs had stuck in the 'almost ready to stand position.' Neither up nor down. We perched for a few minutes in an uncomfortable pose, overjoyed when our porter came to take us to the room. I'm sure it took him five minutes to walk us across reception to the lifts.

The room upgrade was a grateful gift, a rosebud for sure. The suite composed of three large rooms, a further stylish study from the design school of wasted space. The first room had a dining table, complete with six chairs. Why six chairs? There was only one double bed. Who are we expecting to join us for dinner? Three sumptuous leather sofas, positioned around an expanse of glass coffee table, faced a cinema screen of a TV on the wall. Perhaps, if we'd had the cup final of all arguments, finally not speaking to each other, the room would have been ideal. Cosy is not the description.

Entering a dark labyrinth, I find the bathroom is black marble from floor to ceiling. It was, as I imagined and feared, the holy of holies to the god Brand. Not a single item without a hotel monogram. Centre stage holding attention is a bath from the local rugby club. A team of fifteen could get in there with room to swim a few lengths each. To access the local swimming pool was a steep climb, five steps upwards. It would take the tiny taps three hours to gush enough water to dip your toes. We didn't bother.

The bed was the pièce de résistance, a masterpiece of style over function. A wooden sea surrounded an island of mattress. The distance stretched three feet outwards. It created a bed twice the size and half as comfortable. To find sleep requires you to crawl, like a crab, to get to the mattress. Dangling your legs over the edge of the bed was an impossibility, the wood cutting deep in the back of your calf. So you had to be in or out, never in between. Laughing and grateful for the generosity of an 'upgrade,' the practical use of the room took away much of the enjoyment.

Living and travelling by the motto, 'Serendipity favours the brave,' we thought we would have one last stroll. Wandering empty corridors, empty of people and any personality, we reach the rooftop swimming pool. We were alone the entire time. An abandoned hotel. A desert with no oasis in sight. Like we felt in Fort Kochi. The emptiness overflowed the corridors with waves of sadness, as if the hotel was grieving the loss to come. We, and all the people we had visited in Kerala, did not know how big the brewing storm would rage. We closed the door, crawled across the bed, and slept the sleep of a fitful soul.

Snatching at breakfast in a small dining room, the gloom hadn't lifted, but deepened. The absence of any other guests amplified the unnerving restlessness we felt. The hotel courtesy bus transported us the five-minute journey from the echoing silence and emptiness into a two-tone horn screeching red and white barrier taped scene from a disaster movie.

Chaos surrounded the departure terminal entrance, electrified tension replacing the air of empty despair. Fear, and a sense of foreboding, made it a mixture of sheer raw-edged panic clamouring around us. Armed soldiers were checking the passports and tickets of each person entering the terminal. A soldier is blocking the door with his automatic rifle. Stopping us, we can't progress through the doors. I couldn't understand the questions he was asking. The military grade face mask was obscuring his mouth and made his voice sound a mixture between Darth Vader and Gollum. He was getting impatient – I was getting anxious.

Frenzied crowds queued at check-in. It appeared only two foolish people waiting to pass over their cases were not wearing masks. Did we miss the announcement or something? The slightest cough turned heads and shuffled distances. It felt like an exodus. Like a race against time. A rush to get out before 'it' came.

Walking across the skyway from terminal to airplane, I turn to look behind me. A chance for any last glances of India – 'My India' before I board the Emirates flight. The magical, mysterious vibrancy of our trip to Kerala felt it was being washed away in the wave of humanity frantic to leave – me included. I wanted us to leave as well.

Goodbye India.

Chapter 36

No Place Like Home

ARE THERE ARE ROSEBUDS in Kerala? There are. Yes, there are more than I could gather in ten lifetimes It's a proposition I now know to be true – ' posteriori' – it's derived from experience. My experience, 'My India.'

Beautiful, breathtaking, magnificent, and memorable, there are life-changing rosebuds are in Kerala. I brought many back. I left more than I could gather in lifetimes. They filled dusty streets, were stuck on the incense drenched walls of Hindu temples, some danced in the flame of a thousand oil lamps surrounding Lord Krishna's shrine. In the swirls of a thousand saris, to smiles radiating back happiness, and maybe covering sadness, they fed my soul and filled the granaries of my past. I gathered in places and people, also an odd possession or two. I gathered well. I found rosebuds wherever I looked.

I will visit them, meet them, hold them whenever I want, looking forward to my past. Never to be irretrievably lost, each one irrevocably stored and treasured. The granaries of my past are fuller, a part of me forever. Those still young should envy those older like me. Don't give us pity for passing years. We are richer, and our pasts stretch out before us.

The psychiatrist and pioneer in near-death studies, Elisabeth Kubler-Ross, would tell me I could have found as many rosebuds if I stayed at home. She says, 'There is no need to go to India or anywhere else to find peace. You will find that deep place of silence right in your room, your garden or even your bathtub.' She's right and I won't argue with her. There are rosebuds at home.

There is no place like home to gather rosebuds. But here's the difference – the rosebuds I went gathering in Kerala I couldn't have gathered at home. That's why I travel now. There will come a day when I can't. The rosebuds in Kerala changed me, changed the way I see the world, the way I see people, and forever the way I see myself, especially my perspective on the passing of time. On the passing of years. On the passing of my life. The days I spent in Kerala were not deducted from my given lifespan, but add an Indian richness to the future of my past.

Kubler-Ross needn't worry. It was not a search for inner peace, or to 'find myself,' which drew me to India. It was to see if there were any rosebuds there. I wanted to meet the people, catch the immensity of vistas, feel the heartbeat of the country, discovering, experiencing, and swelling the bounty in the 'granaries of my past.'

There are rosebuds in Kerala. And there, as well, is a unique song India sings.

Kerala is a beautiful place. I listen and hear a song that India sings still filling my mind. India, 'My India,' was as magical, chaotic, mysterious, charming, and disturbing as I dreamed – and more.

The song of India is a choir of colour. Nothing about the colours of India is bland – even beige there is striking. Temple garlands for sale are buttery gold, mustard, saffron, and orange. Cascades of every shade of yellow are the marigolds hanging on roadside stalls, anticipating with awe the pinnacle of their existence will be to carry a prayer and bring blessings to the gods. The swatches of the streets are saris, not the notes of red, but the crescendo of fuchsia, primrose, magenta, and burgundy so deep and velvety you could drink it in a glass. Every shade and hue of blues, purples, and greens collided in stanzas sweetly, the melody of the song echoing on every woman and girl.

I catch the song of India played by an orchestral dawn chorus accompanying the rising sun with flutes of prayer. Slapping, snapping drums beat rhythmic greetings to mysterious gods who sit watching in silence. The gods of temples, shrines, and dashboards wove a symphony of faith through our days. Incessant engines throbbing with life, a thumping Royal Enfield, whining tuk-tuks, and rusty creaking bikes. The horn section took front and centre stage, not off to the back and right. The joyous 'rink-a-tink-tink' from the percussion of Bollywood vibrating through saucer-sized speakers emitting visions of darting eyes, backward glances, broken hearts, and lavish dances.

The song of India remains as a beautiful taste. It is the crunch of sweet coconut soaked in coconut milk and doused with rivers of honey. Everest mountains of soft basmati grains and floury dosa accompanied by the inevitable but welcome and accustomed tang of curry leaf. The clean, crisp sweetness of cold Kingfisher beer, beads of sweat running down the bottle. The acrid flavour of diesel suspended on clouds of incense, soaking the air with cinnamon, frankincense, sandalwood, and patchouli. Like a jazz chord sitting unresolved in my mouth, the first cup of brown dust coffee, resting in the mouth unsatisfying, but now lingering delightful with reminisce.

The people I met embodied the song. I'm left curious and confused. Do the multitudes of smiles really hide the sadness in the stories of their lives? If so, there must be a lot of sadness in India. Bright smiles are hard to fake forever, aren't they? Ruled over, kept in place by culture and caste, the people welcomed us with openness and genuine warmth. Not the cursory 'enjoy' when already walking away from the table of our stay, but 'ENJOY!' Embracing our stay with genuine delight, a desire for us to take in the song of India, no matter if its voice was imperceptible above the din of poverty.

The song of India sings loud and clear. Kerala held me captive in every sense. It was impossible for India not to change me. I went to see if there were any rosebuds in Kerala, and I found them. Their song will remain playing, smelling and speaking in my mind for eternity.

I left some song of mine there. I hope front seats of taxis experienced the kindness of strangers as much as the rear. I hope returned smiles and waves passing by through car windows patched a little of the sadness the smiles covered. Often since my return, have I thought about those beautiful people. I wonder how the weeks following our trip changed their world as much as ours changed. As the homestays, hotels, and houseboats would close doors, shut up shop, and moor along silent jetties, how have they fared?

This story was never to be about the pandemic, but the virus will stain for all time everything about 2020. Had our trip began two weeks later, I realise we may not have been able to return home for a significant time.

But return home we did.

There is no place like home.

Chapter 37

Final Homecomings

I am sixty.

My days of fifty-nine and three-quarters have passed into time.

Since time began, humans wanted to measure it. As civilisations stretched over the centuries, creative and elaborate sundials began measuring the passing of time. Minutes into hours – days into weeks – months into years – a lifetime. Sundials fascinate me. It could have been a mere stick in the ground and a few stones in a circle. Who knows how our ancestors learned they could measure time by the movement of the sun?

The practice of inscribing mottos on sundials went hand in hand with the art of designing them. As well as the maker's name, they etched mottos, sayings, and poetry, usually in Latin, in the stone or brass. These thought-provoking words were there to remind those seeking the current hour through the shadow, the days of their life will pass fast-moving as time.

In Saint-Nicolas Catholic church in Saint-Gervais-les-Bains, France, the reflection on mortality on a sundial reads:

EN REGARDANT VOUS VIEILLISSEZ. – Whilst beholding you become old.

Reaching sixty, it's made me ask more 'what if' questions about ageing. What if I turned that around? What if, 'Whilst beholding you become as young?' What if, 'Whilst beholding we become more?'

As we behold the richness of the rosebuds in our lives, we don't become older, but the perspective of our life grows, not diminishes.

Gathering rosebuds in Kerala while moving from fifty-nine and three quarters to sixty, I now see my future differently. I've expanded my view – my longer past is stretching out before me.

Those days and nights amid the sights, sounds, and smells of Southern India added to the richness of my life. They are not lost forever. At sixty, my future is not getting shorter, but it's getting longer.

What if I lived each new day with that changed perspective on growing old? Then each day would be an opportunity to expand my future. The expanse of my life opening up before me, deeper, richer, and more, the future of my past path wide and open until I see a final homecoming is my destination ahead.

Bob Mortimer and Paul Whitehouse are British comedians. Together they embark on various fishing adventures in the BBC series Mortimer and Whitehouse: Gone Fishing. For decades, both made a living, making people smile. There is something else, however, connecting them deeper as friends – both experienced calls far too close with life-threatening illness.

It is sad the weight of worry, and the inconsequential pulls of a materialistic culture which draws us away from what makes a life. It can be a moment of a close call if we experience that, awakening us from a slumber in time to taste the richness of existence. If any good came of the 'Virus' and lockdown days of 2020, maybe the entire world had time to slow down, even a time of a 'close call' – those that lived through it, that is. For those that didn't, their final homecoming was reached sooner and unexpected – as it is for most people.

Bob and Paul live with gratitude each day. The precious gift to keep on living makes them reevaluate, take stock of their lives, laughing and talking about their past lives while waiting for a fish to bite. The places they fish, and the beautiful photography of those locations, along with a stunning soundtrack to match, make it one of my favourite TV shows to watch.

I snigger at their antics, catch a lump in my throat and tears in my eye as they watch a river run by, revealing a genuine friendship and love of spending time together. The Greeks called it 'Philia,' genuine love between friends. We have perhaps lost something of the depth of friendship between male friends; 'bromance' robs the authentic depths of trust and openness, reducing vulnerability to a cliche. If I'm honest, I envy that relationship they have. Distance and circumstance rob me of that opportunity to spend time with two close male friends I have.

By riverbank and pool Bob and Paul chat about their life – the hardships of loss, the fleeting transience of fame, how what once seemed important is now fading, the preciousness of regaining time with the people they love now taking prime place. Among the laughter and teasing are moments of immense poignancy that wouldn't be out of place in a philosophical documentary as they reflect on the random and unexplainable facets of life. You could call the programme – Mortimer and Whitehouse: Gone Gathering Rosebuds.

The last episode of season three finds Bob and Paul fishing for chub on the River Wye. Brilliant white swans drift by, their flexible necks tucking deep into wing feathers, shielding them from razor-sharp rays of sunlight. Bob gets down on his hands and knees, exclaiming how extraordinary the perspective of the river is from that angle.

'What do you think amounts to a worthwhile life?' he asks Paul. Bob tells of a recent visit to his 85-year-old father-in-law's house and sees how he has been using Google Maps to revisit the places of his life where he lived or where he had a lovely time. Bob thinks it was like his father-in-law was collecting up all his memories one last time, before he moved on to 'wherever we go with a nice collection of memories.' Then he ponders the idea some more. 'What if we arrive at the 'next place' with a lovely bag of memories, reunited with those we have lost? Perhaps then you can share each other's bag of memories?' he asks.

What if that is true? How extraordinary is the perspective of our future from that angle?

How beautiful is such a path to our future? Our final homecoming, 'wherever we go,' will be to walk for all time among the rosebuds we have gathered in the granaries of our past. But not to walk alone. I cherish that perspective now I have reached sixty. Paul discounted it as just a lovely metaphor. What if he is wrong?

What if, as we are moving forward in time, its destination is to the palaces of the past? That too is not a typo – not places, but palaces. To the life we lived and the riches that filled it? What if we are moving towards a 'next place,' our final homecoming, and the destination is the granaries of our pasts? Those storehouses filled with the rosebuds of our lives? What a final homecoming that would be! It is an extraordinary perspective on how to see our life.

Why did Charles Foster Kane, played by Orson Welles in his epic film Citizen Kane, murmur the word on his deathbed: 'Rosebud?' Was it a flashback, 'life passing before his eyes,' as if the scenes of his years were being played out for an ultimate time, an infinite moment in a finite life? Do we, close to death, unload all the 'rosebud' memories of our life?

I live with a blessing and gratitude to have travelled well through life – but more, more I have an ultimate home to travel towards. One day I will be in that home, without the need to travel again. 'Life passing before my eyes' or not.

What if our last homecoming is to be the opportunity to spend eternity, or forever time, wandering those granaries of our pasts forever? Sauntering here and there, reliving those moments, experiencing our gathered rosebud moments without end. It would make gathering rosebuds today a vital activity. It sounds sentimental; I understand. But it also sounds a lot like heaven to me.

It takes around two weeks for a rosebud to bloom into a flower. A rosebud is a visual promise a beautiful flower will grow. A future splendour hidden within the folds, waiting for the moment to realise its true potential. You can't rush it. You can't unfold it too soon to see the beauty before its time is ready.

What if our lifetime collection of rosebuds is like a puzzle – all the separate pieces turned out on the table, a mixture of peeping colour amongst the cardboard grey? It's only when the puzzle is complete that all the randomness of life makes sense?

What if rosebuds make up a Magic Eye puzzle of our life? It's only when you stand back and focus you get to see the beauty of it all? The longer you look, the clearer the view becomes? Until you can no longer 'see through a glass darkly', but arriving at our final homecoming we can see it all?

What if we do get the opportunity to reunite with those we have loved and show them around the granaries of our years? The blooms of our life lived now in full colour.

Hello dad, I've missed you. I was fifteen when I last saw you. I want to share with you so many wonderful memories. My life? Dad, it's been a daring adventure for me, not nothing. I hope you are proud of how I lived it. No, I never got to wear a deerstalker like you.

Hey, dad, come with me. Let me show the moment that your son got married to the love of his life. She's called Noreen. There's no rush, we can stay a while here and relive that day in slow motion. It snowed that day. Let's rewind that beautiful day over and over.

Dad, I want to take you over to the day when your granddaughter was born. We can experience the beauty of her new life again. I want to show you too, dad; you have a grandson. When he was born, he had ginger hair, just like yours!

The indomitable spirit you had, the way you saw life being a daring adventure or nothing courses through their veins – your passion for life is in their life. Travel, writing, adventure, and fun – you passed all that on as well.

In writing this book and taking time to consider deeper my days in Kerala, being present in this moment is one of the most precious gifts I can give myself. It is what Eckhart Tolle calls, 'The collective disease of humanity.' Absorbed by the content of our life, we forget the essence. We miss the now. We can be 'so consumed by time that they have forgotten eternity, which is their origin, their home, their destiny.' Distraction robs the opportunity to gather a rosebud – the worse affliction of that is digital distraction. I'm trying to 'let go' of the persistent need to always be 'connected' to the world when being 'connected' to the culture results in being disconnected from my life now.

My friend Paul inspired me to document my days in Kerala. He is an inspiration and the inspiration for my asking the question – 'Are there Rosebuds in Kerala?' His simple suggestion was to write the stories down as I sent him email updates on my travels. I'm thankful he did. That nudge made me look closer at each day, to pay more attention, to be fully present in this moment. In 'Crossing To Safety,' a novel by Wallace Stegner, he reminds how, 'being close to the mortality of friends, you are brought to think of your own.' What a gift Paul gave to me. This book is my gift to him. Thank you Paul.

I didn't need to go to Kerala to gather rosebuds, but I am glad I did. Though unexpected and unwanted, the world changed forever in the time it took for me to get from fifty-nine and three quarters to sixty.

I am grateful for each day I have, and grateful for however many remain. To say the thought of how many days remain for me never fills my mind would not be true. Writing about people who have died brings me alongside the painful loss of others. I accompany families to the rough torn edges of grief and loss weekly, the privileged process reminding me of the mortality of those I love – and mine as well. Looking forward to the future with the perspective of life expanding as I move towards my past soothes this realisation. The perspective of my life from that angle is extraordinary. It took me to travel to Kerala, and reach sixty, to understand the best way to live life is to view it backwards.

Here I am facing my sixth decade standing firmly in the present, with my back to the future, with my eyes scanning the rosebuds of my past. This perspective of ageing helps find past answers to present day questions. My future unknown is behind me, while my past is ahead, rich in memories of rosebuds gathered. I'm left inspired to live this day, to make the most of this moment, to be present, but to be on the search. Ready.

I'm off to gather more 'rosebuds' while I may.

After all, life really is a 'daring adventure or nothing.'

The End

Acknowledgements

THANK YOU NOREEN, MY wife and my rosebud gathering travel companion. Life has blessed us to sojourn together across the globe. But even if we'd never left home, I'm so grateful we have been blessed to travel through life together for many years. You are the essence and fragrance of a rosebud to me. Thank you for giving me time and space to write the first scrappy drafts, and then having enough patience to read them! Thank you for the times you have let me go on adventures, and always being there welcoming me home. I love you very much.

I can see in you, Sam and Laura, my spirit of living a daring adventure, but just as much your Grandad Sid's. I am so proud of you both in all you do. Now our family includes you, Graham – a man with a heart of expedition and adventure just as much. I'm grateful for the places you three have all travelled so far. Long may that wanderlust burn, never diminished. Thank you for keeping it burning in me.

Thank you, Laura, for reading drafts and offering so many thoughtful ideas posed as questions. It made me search deeper for meanings, illustrations, and showing me the places I need to tell less and show more. I'm sure I haven't got that correct ... yet. Writing a book is harder and takes longer than you can ever believe but is more rewarding than I could imagine. Much of this book would not have been possible without your help, thank you.

Thanks Alex Davis for guiding me to restructure the first draft. Thank you for the extremely hard, patient work of editing of my misuse of grammar and misspelling. Hail to the 'single' rather than "double" quotes!

Allwyn and Jency, you were so willing and generous to tell me your story of how love conquered over the challenges you faced. It is such a privilege and honour you have given me the permission to share your story in this book. I am very grateful and hope that we may meet again one day.

For many years, Sheri Saginor and Craig Miller, you have been a source of encouragement, support and wisdom during our regular 'Mastermind' calls. We have travelled the roads of TED talks, Smart Speeches and Death Going Digital. What an adventure together we've shared ... and more to come! Thank you for encouraging me to persist in the writing of this book.

There are friends who stay closer than a brother. To my 'life-time' friend, Terry Bennett, thank you. The 'granaries of our pasts' are full of gathered rosebuds. We have journeyed over mountains, sailed stormy waters, laughed till we cried, cried until we could cry no more. What a blessing from Him who brought our lives together all those many years ago. Thanks Terry.

Thank you Larry Kineman, my 'Camino Buddy' and friend. Apart from sharing hundreds of miles walking across France and Spain, we have shared so many years of life together. There are rosebuds aplenty gathered ready for us to saunter through again one day – you, me and Geronimo. I'm grateful for your input on early drafts of the book, and for your unconditional friendship.

Thank you to several local funeral directors, and funeral arrangers, who recommend me as a celebrant. I never take for granted the trust and confidence placed in me by your introductions to the families you serve. It is an honour to write the words of a eulogy for their loved ones. In particular, I would like to say thank you to Julie-Julie, Vanda, and Ben. During a period of writing this book when I experienced personal challenges, filled with many ups and downs, your frequent calls and regular emails 'checking-in' on me made such a difference to my life. I will be forever grateful to you for your care.

Susana, Michael, Dan, Johnny, and Neville, you have helped me shape thoughts and ideas around titles and sales pages. Thank you for the input, encouragement, and holding me to pursue words, phrases, and sentences, mining each clause, till cutting and polishing them they become gems.

Thank you Pippa – 'the office dog,' my faithful friend, and morning coffee companion. While some dogs are trained to sniff out truffles or contraband, you can smell a rosebud in a flash – that and a gravy bone biscuit in my pocket. You've listened well to my rambling.

And to Dad and Mom, thank you most of all – because without you two, I wouldn't have been able to do any of this incredible life. Till we can wander through the granaries of our pasts together.

About The Author

Peter Billingham is a highly recognised and Google 5 star reviewed eulogy writer. After writing over 700 eulogies, his 'story-centred' approach creates memorable words that capture the essence of a loved one. Listening to hundreds of life stories, Peter understands deeply those moments that make our lives memorable.

Peter is the author of Nailed To The Cross, Death Goes Digital, and several funeral industry magazine articles. His newsletter, The Art of Memorialisation, many see as a leading source of news, opinion and trends on Digital Legacy, Online Memorials, and #Deathtech.

His passion for travel is unabated. The joy of packing a suitcase has seen him visit forty-one countries so far for pleasure and in working across the world for an international charity. He hasn't given up on the idea of a 'Gap Year' yet!

You can find out more about Peter Billingham at www.peter-billingham.com

CHAPTER 38

GATHERING ROSEBUDS WEBSITE

FREE COPY OF GATHERING ROSEBUDS - THE WORKBOOK & WORKSHEETS

As a way of saying 'Thank You' for buying a print version of my book, I would like to give you a copy of - Gathering Rosebuds - The Workbook and a 42 page PDF with worksheets for each of the three phases I explain in the process of gathering rosebuds in your life.

To obtain your free download of these resources go to:

https://gatheringrosebuds.co.uk/freeworkbook/

Gathering Rosebuds is a website of resources. You will find there several tools and encouragement to enable you to bring together, memory by memory, rosebud by rosebud, until you are harvesting a storehouse of your life's special moments.

What will you find at Gathering Rosebuds?

- Workbooks, Cards, Posters, & Journals
- Video Courses, Audio books, & Podcasts

- Photo galleries from the book – *Gathering Rosebuds in Kerala*

If you have enjoyed reading the book, you'll treasure taking the next step forward.

Please consider leaving a review on Amazon!

I hope that you enjoyed *Gathering Rosebuds In Kerala*. It would mean the world to me if you have enjoyed this workbook to leave a review online. It's how the world is these days! What other people have enjoyed influences our choices. By writing a few lines about what you enjoyed and how it helped you start to curate your life you can help me so much. Thank you.

> '*The things we do outlast our mortality. The things we do are like monuments that people build to honour heroes after they've died. They're like the pyramids that the Egyptians built to honour the pharaohs. Only instead of being made of stone, they're made out of the memories people have of you.*' **R.J. Palacio**

About Randan Press

RANDAN PRESS IS NOT a publishing house, publishing agent, or company. All our books we self-publish through KDP (Kindle Direct Publishing), IngramSpark, and similar book self-publishing platforms.

Randan Press is the pen name we use to self-publish books in our family. Why? The name and logo have a significant connection to my father.

For several reasons, Dad turned to writing to make a living, and writing was good to him at the time he needed it. Honing his craft on a portable Smith Corona typewriter, I remember the sound of its keys snapping forward, the ink on my fingers betraying the evidence I had been 'fiddling' with it (as he called it).

I wish I could write books by pressing on those keys today.

Dad taught himself journalism and magazine article writing. Dad would attend trade shows for the HVAC industry. Then write articles, press releases and longer form editorials. With his self belief in his ability, plus incredible work ethic, he made a living.

Dad's writing DNA is in all the family. It's in our blood. Dad understood what it took to be a writer. His influence is in this book, many other books already published, and in time to publish under the name Randan Press.

I wanted to acknowledge Dad in all our writing. The pen-name Randan Press is my way of doing that to honour his memory.

Thanks Dad.

Disclaimer

This book is a memoir, a work of creative non-fiction. While all the incidents described in this book are true, it may not be entirely factual. It portrays the events to the best of the author's memory and recollections, compressing certain events, consolidating, or reordering others, to ensure continuity of the narrative.

The names and identifying details of most people in this book were changed or omitted. This is to protect the identities and privacy of individuals involved, apart from where it was possible to request permission and a release granted. In order to maintain anonymity, sometimes, the names of locations have been changed and many left out. Also changed are some identifying characteristics and details such as the physical properties and places of residence to provide and protect privacy.

Non-fiction is mostly written from memory. All conversations in the book are as close an approximation as possible to actual conversations that took place, to the best of the author's recollection. They are not word-for-word transcripts. Rather, the author has retold them in a way that evokes the feeling and meaning of what was said and, in all instances, the essence of the dialogue is accurate.

All logos, trademarks and registered trademarks are the property of their respective owners.

The reader should not consider this book anything other than a work of creative non-fiction literature.

Any external website links are only for reference. Content from any such articles may have changed or removed without the author's knowledge. Links to free downloads and book offers are not guaranteed to be accessible in perpetuity. The author will try to correct errors brought to their attention.

Printed in Great Britain
by Amazon

33487328R00166